Sequencer Secrets

Sequencer Secrets

Ian Waugh

PC Publishing

PC Publishing
Export House
130 Vale Road
Tonbridge
Kent TN9 1SP
UK
Tel 01732 770893
Fax 01732 770268
email pcp@cix.compulink.co.uk
website http://www.pc-pubs.demon.co.uk

First published 1995, reprinted 1997

© PC Publishing

ISBN 1 870775 37 6

British Library Cataloguing in Publication Data

A catalogue record for this book is available from the British Library

Printed and bound in Great Britain by BPC Wheatons Ltd, Exeter

Contents

Acknowledgments

Although I am responsible for committing these tips to paper, I did not devise all the ideas alone. Some tips came from discussions with sequencer software developers, others came from demonstrators whose job it is to present their product in the best possible light, others came from discussions with studio musicians and sequencer users and yes, some I believe I did discover myself.

So a big Thank You to all the sequencer users who have, consciously or unconsciously, contributed to this book.

 *Dedication*

To Julia, for making me realise that there is more to life than
sequencing...

Introduction

This book contains a collection of sequencer tips, tricks and ideas which I have acquired working with a wide range of sequencers over many years.

Modern sequencers have an enormous number of functions. The manual may explain what the functions do but not many tell you how to use them in a practical, musical way. In some ways this is understandable, for to include practical examples with each function would undoubtedly double the size of the manual – and how many people read the manual thoroughly, anyway?

But nestling inside the screens and menus of your sequencer are dozens of functions which can be used in all manner of ways. Unlike a manual which tells you what the functions do, this book tells you how to use them in musical and practical ways. Not to explore these functions is to severely under-use the potential of your sequencer.

The tips cover a wide range of topics from setting up your system to turning your multi-event, multi-track digital sequencer into an analogue sequencer! How's that for progress?

The tips are divided into groups for easy reference and there is a comprehensive index so if you need to do some work with controllers, for example, you will easily be able to find the relevant tips. Some ideas could well fit into two sections but this shouldn't cause any confusion.

Some of the tips involve entering or modifying data in your sequencer. As this involves you actually *doing* something, we've called them projects and flagged them with this sign – ☑ *PROJECT.*

The majority of the tips are not specific to any particular sequencer although, of course, many tips rely on the fact that a sequencer has certain facilities such as a delay function or a graphic controller editor. The tips assume that you know how to use your sequencer and have a basic understanding of MIDI. In order to cram in as many ideas as possible, many tips are quite short and to the point. If you need basic sequencing tuition, you've picked up the wrong book!

You'll get most out of this book if you read it from start to finish, but it has been designed for the busy sequencer user so feel free to dip into it when the occasion demands. Many of the suggestions are designed to get you thinking in a more lateral direction.

I'm aware that keyboards aren't the only fruit – or MIDI recording device for that matter – but the majority of sequencer users are keyboard-based. With deference to that fact I write with the assumption that the user is using a keyboard for recording (except in those sections dedicated to a specific instrument) but acknowledge that they may well be using something else.

Finally, don't forget that the ultimate aim of using a sequencer is to produce great music. Don't confuse technology with creativity.

❏ Your best tips

A book such as this can never be complete. There are always more hints and tips waiting to be discovered, especially as sequencers are updated and acquire more functions, and as users become more adventurous.

If you have a sequencer tip, send it along. If we consider it worthy of inclusion in the second edition we'll send you a £10 voucher towards the cost of any book (or books) from the PC Publishing range – you won't have to wait until the second edition comes out!

We prefer the tips to be general and applicable to all sequencers but if there is sufficient demand – and response – we will consider including sections of tips for individual sequencers.

Tips must be typed or very neatly written. Please say which sequencer and computer you use and include a MIDI file if it helps explain your idea more clearly. We regret we are unable to return submissions. Send to:

Sequencer Secrets Tips
PC Publishing
Export House
130 Vale Road
Tonbridge
Kent TN9 1SP
UK

2 Setting up your system

We'll start with the tip you'll like least! Even though you hate the thought of it, read your sequencer's manual from cover to cover at least once! The more you know what it can do, the more easily its functions will fall under your fingers. Check out its more esoteric functions which you haven't yet explored such as data manipulation and transformation functions.

❏ Register

Register your software. Lots of people don't so they never find out about bug fixes, updates, special offers and so on. Also, you may have to register before you can get technical support from the distributor. You know it makes sense!

❏ Having a preference

Many sequencers automatically load a file called Autoload, Prefs or Setup which contains settings such as MIDI port assignments, instrument lists, track parameters and so on. Customise this and use it to save setting up time each time you start a new project.

If your sequencer doesn't load a Prefs file, create a blank song containing your preferred settings and load it after booting your sequencer. But don't forget to save it straight away again using the name of the new song otherwise you'll overwrite the original! This is bound to happen at least once so create a backup copy of your Prefs song.

Create several Pref files for different projects and equipment – one for working with a General MIDI instrument, one with tracks transposed for orchestral scores, one set up for external synchronisation and so on. Many sequencers come with a selection of files for just such purposes so see what's hidden in some of those nested folders you never looked at since installing your sequencer.

❏ Preferences on the Mac

If you are using an Apple Mac you can turn a file into a Stationery document by highlighting the file, selecting Get Info from the File menu and checking the Stationery box. You can load your sequencer and this file by double-clicking on it but when you try to save it you will be prompted for a new file name. Some sequencers may copy the file before loading it which has a similar effect.

Creating a Stationery document on the Mac to use as a Preferences file.

❏ MIDI Thru

Most sequencers have a soft MIDI Thru setting and it's worth getting to know how it works. Essentially, it's like the Thru socket on an instrument and passes signals arriving at the computer's In socket back through its Out socket. However, rather than pass the exact same signal out, most sequencers have a channelise function which will transmit the incoming data back out on the MIDI channel of the currently-selected track. Let's see how this works.

In the old days, standard practice was to set your keyboard to channel 1, record a part, select another track, set the transmit channel to 2 and record another part and so on. If you set up MIDI Thru correctly there will be no need to change the transmit channel on your keyboard.

In practice you would set each track to a different MIDI channel and assign the sounds in your keyboard or expander to different MIDI channels. Many users find it useful to assign track one to MIDI channel one and so on although if you are creating a General MIDI file you may prefer to adopt the GM channel format.

To hear the sound assigned to channel four, for example, you would simply select or highlight track four and play your keyboard.

There are a couple of things you need to be aware of. If you are using your keyboard for playback rather than a sound module and if the Thru is transmitting on the same channel your keyboard is transmitting on you may hear double notes – the ones generated when you physically play the keyboard and their 'ghosts' arriving from the sequencer.

The sound of some electric pianos, for example, may seem to be doing strange things with the harmonics. Some sounds and instruments will be affected more than others. Apart from sounding strange, this will half the polyphony of your keyboard and is generally to be avoided.

You can avoid it in one of two ways. The simplest is to switch off Local Control on your keyboard. This disconnects the keys from the sound production section so you only hear what is (re)transmitted from the sequencer. Do this when using other synths or expanders, too, so you won't hear the keyboard along with the expander's sound. Not all keyboards have a Local Control function, however.

Some sequencers have an alternative which lets you select a channel which MIDI Thru WILL NOT transmit on. In this case you set it to the channel your master keyboard is transmitting on.

Once you sort out your Thrus, you'll find that the process of sequencing becomes easier. It's well worth spending a little time to get it right.

Notator lets you specify a MIDI channel which will NOT be transmitted through the Out socket.

❑ Metronome click

You need a metronome click so you can play in time. Many sequencers let you assign different volumes or even different sounds to the first beat of the bar and subdivisions of the beat. This is very helpful, particularly with compound time signatures such as 6/8 and 12/8.

If you are recording a piece at a slow tempo, use subdivisional clicks to help keep you in time. Many musicians have a tendency to push or drag at slow tempos.

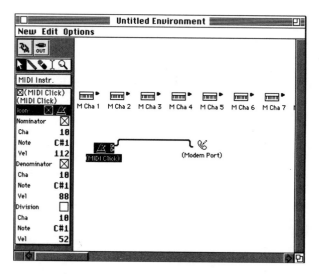

Logic's sophisticated MIDI Click lets you set different notes, MIDI channels and velocities for the nominator, denominator and beat subdivision.

❑ A better metronome

Playing to a click is all very well, even an accented one, but how much better to play along with a drum track. Record a simple drum pattern in the style of the song you are writing and copy it several dozen times to create a long click track.

You'll find this far easier to follow than a metronome click and it will give you a better feel when composing new parts. At least one sequencer now actually uses a drum track as a metronome.

❑ Do you need a Thru box or MIDI Switcher?

If you have more than two synths or expanders you can usually connect them together by daisy chaining. This involves connecting the MIDI Thru of one instrument to the MIDI In of another and connecting that one's MIDI Thru to another instrument's MIDI In and so on.

The MIDI Thru socket passes on a copy of the data arriving at the In socket. It's important to realise that it does not transmit any data which the instrument itself generates. MIDI Thru is there purely to allow MIDI messages to be passed around a system.

However, daisy chain routing is totally inflexible and if you daisy chain several instruments you may experience problems. In particular, the signal may deteriorate or become distorted which could result in the loss of data. Apart from all that, not all instruments have a MIDI Thru socket.

Some authorities believe that daisy chaining can delay the signal. The delay caused by going from MIDI In to MIDI Thru is only a few millionths of a second which is certainly not audible. A Thru delay in a modern instrument should be very rare although some older ones with a less efficient MIDI interface may cause a problem. See 'The truth about MIDI delay' in the Troubleshooting section for more info.

A MIDI Thru box and/or a MIDI Switcher can save a lot of time and effort. But which one is for you?

A Thru box will take one MIDI signal, say from your sequencer, and transmit it to several instruments. A MIDI switcher lets you change the way your instruments are connected together. You could, for example, route the MIDI In of a sound module to your sequencer and then, by flicking a switch, route it to your keyboard.

To save voice data from a module to your sequencer you must be able to connect its Out to the sequencer's In. If the sequencer's In is normally connected to your keyboard's Out you'll need a MIDI switcher to do the repatching.

The optimum solution will depend on your equipment and setup but if you find yourself constantly fiddling around at the back of your equipment repatching leads you know it's time for some sort of patching and routing system.

The most flexible solution is to use a Thru box to channel playback from a sequencer to all your sound modules and a switcher to select different routings when required.

Philip Rees produces an excellent range of budget-priced MIDI routing boxes and has a very helpful catalogue which shows the benefits of different types of MIDI box.

❏ Do you need a MIDI merger?

Unlike audio signals, you can't mix MIDI data by twisting together a couple of MIDI leads. MIDI signals are digital and often consist of two or three bytes or packets of information which must be kept together. A MIDI merger accepts two or more signals and interleaves them using a microprocessor to do the analysis so the packets aren't split up.

If you want to control a unit from two different sources you need a MIDI merger. One common application is with voice editing software where you need to transmit to a sound module from the computer during editing and from a keyboard so you can play the sound.

You would also use a MIDI merger if you wanted to record into your sequencer or play a sound module from two separate MIDI controllers – two keyboards, a keyboard and a MIDI guitar, or a keyboard and set of drum pads, for example.

You need to ensure that the merger supports MTC (MIDI Time Code) correctly and Sys Ex messages. Philip Rees produces an excellent MIDI merger which also sums pitch bend data arriving on the same MIDI channel, helping to avoid pitch bend conflicts. It also supports Running Status. See the 'Easing MIDI delay problems' in the Troubleshooting section for more about Running Status.

Philip Rees MIDI merge units

❑ 32 MIDI channels

If you have more than one sound module, MIDI's 16 channels can soon become a limitation. This is especially true if you are using a General MIDI module which automatically responds to data on all 16 MIDI channels and also want to use a synth.

In such a case you cannot use the GM unit in tandem with another instrument unless you resort to physical tricks such as creating a sequence to set the volume levels of the channels you don't want the GM module to play to 0 and playing it without the other instrument connected. Not conducive to creative sequencing, I'm sure you'll agree.

However, before we continue, it's worth pointing out that not all GM modules automatically respond to every MIDI channel and some do allow individual channels to be switched off. Also some let you do this using Sys Ex messages so take a close look at the MIDI Data Format section of your GM modules' manual.

But even with traditional synths and samplers, an additional 16 MIDI channels will increase your polyphony, cut down on potential MIDI timing problems, allow you to play MIDI guitar parts in mono mode (if you don't have a MIDI guitar you can ignore this!) and generally give you more scope for arranging and organising your music.

You can buy MIDI interfaces for most sequencers and computers which contain multiple MIDI sockets. Most of these are relatively expensive, although they may also have synchronisation facilities or other functions. However, if all you want is more MIDI channels there are cheaper alternatives.

For example, on the Atari ST, Emagic's Notator, Steinberg's Cubase and Software's Technology's Breakthru Plus to name but three can access another 16 channels using a device such as ModemMIDI which plugs into the ST's modem/serial port. These cost less than £30 and are available from various suppliers including Club Cubase.

On the Mac you can connect a MIDI interface to the modem or printer port – or both – and most Mac sequencers enable you to assign a track to a port as well as a MIDI channel. You can, therefore, access another 16 MIDI channels by buying a cheap MIDI interface and plugging it into the other Mac port, although do make sure your sequencer can support two ports, first.

You can plug two MIDI interfaces into a PC – but make sure the internal settings are not going to clash.

❑ Monitor mania

The standard monitor for most computers is 14" and most PC users, for example, probably use a resolution of 640 x 480. However, many modern sequencers are designed around a series of windows and a larger monitor running at a higher resolution will let you see more of the sequencer on screen at any one time.

Yes, they're more expensive but a 15" monitor is not much more and it will give you a noticeably-larger desktop which will make working with windows easier.

In any event, make the maximum use of your monitor by making the windows fill as much of the screen as possible.

Working practices

❏ Hot keys

The advantage of using a mouse and a GUI (Graphic User Interface) is that you don't have to remember lots of keyboard commands. But keystrokes are far quicker and most sequencers have several functions which can only be accessed from the keyboard.

At the very least you should learn the keys for starting and stopping your sequencer. Make a point of learning two or three new commands each time you use your sequencer and you'll be surprised how much faster you work. A good ploy is to copy out or photocopy the section of the manual which lists the hot keys and stick it on the wall next to your monitor.

Key Commands	
☒ Record	Global Commands
Key	'+' Record
Modifier ⇧	'*' Record Repeat
Learn Key	Space Record Toggle
	'0' Play
	',' Pause
	Enter Stop
	⌘Left Rewind
	⌘Right Forward
	⇧ ⌘Left Fast Rewind
	⇧ ⌘Right Fast Forward
	≺ Left Scrub Rewind
	≺ Right Scrub Forward
	Start from Beginning
	Start from Left Locator
	Start from Right Locator
	Set Locators & Play
	'=' Set rounded Locators & Play
	Set rounded Locators & Play & Cycle
	≺ 'c' Cycle
	≺ 'd' Drop
	Replace
	≺ 's' Solo
	Sync intern/extern
	Tape Control Mode
	Set next higher Format
	Set next lower Format
	MIDI Click
	Help Send Reset Controllers
	Send discrete Note Offs (FullPanic)
	≺ 'v' Send Maximum Volume
	Send Used Instruments MIDI Settings

Notator Logic has on-line help for all its hot key commands.

❏ Taking note

If your sequencer has a Notepad – use it! Make notes about the song you are creating and include details of all external equipment, how they are connected and their settings. You may think you'll remember it all but I can guarantee you won't! If your sequencer doesn't have a Notepad – use your wordprocessor and create an Info file to accompany each song. You'll thank me for this piece of advice one day...

❏ Mighty mouse

To speed up operation of your sequencer – and all your other applications, too – increase the speed of the mouse using the computer's built-in mouse utility (found in the Control Panel on the Mac and PC) or a utility for the ST such as Mouse Accelerator.

If it feels strange at first and the mouse pointer zooms off the edge of the screen, practice – you'll soon get used to it and it will greatly improve your efficiency.

You can alter the Mouse settings on a PC from the Control Panel in Windows.

❏ Dialling the right program number

Some sequencers use program change numbers from 0 to 127 which is correct according to MIDI because computers start counting at 0 and not 1. Others use the range 1 to 128 which is more user-friendly.

Similar variations occur with synthesisers so check that the two numbering systems match up. If they don't, you'll have to add or subtract 1 from the program change number you use in your sequencer in order to select the required sound.

❏ Banking on it

Some instruments arrange their sounds in banks so instead of numbering them from 1 to 128 they may have, say, eight banks named A to G each containing 16 sounds. In such a case, MIDI program number 33, for example, would select the sound in bank C2.

If you have an instrument which organises its sounds in banks, make a list of the program numbers your sequencer uses and write down the bank numbers each one selects. This will save a lot of time.

❑ Bank select

Most modern instruments – and many older ones, too – have more than 128 sounds so MIDI's standard 128 program change numbers is simply not enough to access them all from a sequencer. In 1990 the Bank Select message was added to the MIDI spec and this will switch a synthesiser to a new bank of sounds providing it supports the Bank Select message. (This is for instruments with more than 128 sounds, not for those with 128 sounds which have been arranged into banks.)

The MIDI spec uses two controllers, 0 and 32, each capable of selecting 128 banks – that's an amazing total of 16,384 banks! As each bank can hold 128 sounds that's a potential of 2,097,152 sounds! It's unlikely that any manufacturer will produce an instrument with sounds in excess of this number, at least during the next 12 months! Consider, if it took only one second to listen to a sound, it would take over three weeks working 24 hours a day to listen to each one. Still, you never know what's cooking in America and Japan.

Back in the real world, several sequencers now directly support the Bank Select message and let you enter a Bank Select number much as you enter a program number. If your sequencer doesn't allow this, you can enter the Bank Select data directly into your sequencer's event list. Controller 32 is used to select banks 0 to 127. Check if your instruments support Bank Select messages by looking at their MIDI Implementation Charts.

Notator Logic lets you select Banks from the Instrument Parameter box.

❑ GS Bank Select

Roland's GS Bank Select format uses a slightly different system to that of the MIDI spec. It uses a single MIDI controller, 0, to specify a bank range of 0 to 127. Make sure you use the correct selection system for your instruments.

❑ GS Bank Select with Notator Logic

Emagic's Notator Logic lets you select Bank Select messages directly in the instrument parameters box. It defaults to the MIDI spec system but it can also be used to select sounds in GS banks.

To make Logic use the GS Bank Select format, go to the Environment page, create a Multi Instrument, double click on it to bring up its parameter window and select Control 0 for the Bank Select parameter.

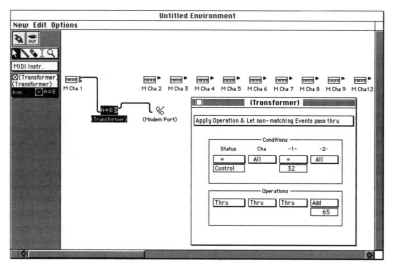

(Multi Instr.)					
Device Name			Short Device Name		
(Multi Instr.)					
(No Bank specified. Names of Bank 0 used)			Bank Message: Control 32 ▼		

Program Name				Bank Message: Control 0		
Prg 0=11	Prg 16=31	Prg 32=51	Prg 48=71	Prg 6 Control 32 without MSB		
Prg 1=12	Prg 17=32	Prg 33=52	Prg 49=72	Prg 6 Control 0 without LSB		
Prg 2=13	Prg 18=33	Prg 34=53	Prg 50=73	Prg 6 Ensoniq VFX, SD-1: 2xPrg		
Prg 3=14	Prg 19=34	Prg 35=54	Prg 51=74	Prg 6 TG 500: +32 (Ctrl 32)		
Prg 4=15	Prg 20=35	Prg 36=55	Prg 52=75	Prg 6 JV-80/880: +80 (Ctrl 0)		
Prg 5=16	Prg 21=36	Prg 37=56	Prg 53=76	Prg 6 Kurzweil K1000/K1200		
Prg 6=17	Prg 22=37	Prg 38=57	Prg 54=77	Prg 7 Yamaha TG77 (Prg 117...)		
Prg 7=18	Prg 23=38	Prg 39=58	Prg 55=78	Prg 7 Oberheim Matrix 1000		
Prg 8=21	Prg 24=41	Prg 40=61	Prg 56=81	Prg 72	Prg 88	Prg 104	Prg 120
Prg 9=22	Prg 25=42	Prg 41=62	Prg 57=82	Prg 73	Prg 89	Prg 105	Prg 121
Prg 10=23	Prg 26=43	Prg 42=63	Prg 58=83	Prg 74	Prg 90	Prg 106	Prg 122
Prg 11=24	Prg 27=44	Prg 43=64	Prg 59=84	Prg 75	Prg 91	Prg 107	Prg 123
Prg 12=25	Prg 28=45	Prg 44=65	Prg 60=85	Prg 76	Prg 92	Prg 108	Prg 124
Prg 13=26	Prg 29=46	Prg 45=66	Prg 61=86	Prg 77	Prg 93	Prg 109	Prg 125
Prg 14=27	Prg 30=47	Prg 46=67	Prg 62=87	Prg 78	Prg 94	Prg 110	Prg 126
Prg 15=28	Prg 31=48	Prg 47=68	Prg 63=88	Prg 79	Prg 95	Prg 111	Prg 127

You can use the GM or GS method of bank selection in Notator Logic.

❏ Accessing more banks in Notator Logic

The maximum Bank Select number allowed by Logic is 62. If banks in instruments were numbered consecutively you probably wouldn't need to access that many but, for various reasons, they aren't.

To access banks higher than 62, create a Transformer in the Environment page, double click on it to call up its parameters, set the Status box in Conditions to Control and the -1- box to 0 or 32 depending on whether you're using the MIDI spec or the GS spec.

Using Logic's Transform function to access bank numbers greater than 62.

Set the first three Operations to Thru but change the last one to Add. In the box below Add insert the number by which you want to increment the bank number.

For example, if you were using the MIDI system and wanted to select bank 127, you would set the -1- box to 32 and the value below the Add box to 65. The Transformer will then add 65 to Logic's maximum bank range of 62 (62 + 65 = 127).

Before this will work you have to patch the Transformer into the system by connecting the output from an Instrument to the Transformer's input and connecting the Transformer's output to the modem or serial port, whichever one the MIDI interface is connected to. If you're not a Logic user this probably won't make much sense but if you are a Logic user, hopefully it will.

❑ Bank Select and Procyon Pro

The bank function in Procyon uses Controller 0 in the range 0-127 and is directly compatible with GS instruments. If you need to use the GM method insert Controller 32 messages in the Event Editor.

❑ Earlier Bank Select methods

Before the Bank Select message entered the MIDI spec, manufacturers developed their own way of changing banks. One method, implemented on Yamaha's SY77 and Kurzweil's 1000 and 1200 series, for example, was to use two consecutive program change numbers. The first would switch the bank and the second would select the sound in it. The SY77, for example, uses values over 64 to select a bank. Each bank only holds 64 sounds so values below this are used to select sounds. If you have an instrument which works like this insert the relevant program change numbers in the Event Editor.

❑ Patch lists

Many modern sequencers let you select sounds by name rather than using program change and bank numbers. This saves an awful lot of time and is especially useful with GM and GS instruments.
However, if you're working with programmable instruments you may find yourself in a chicken and egg situation. You probably won't decide on the final selection of sounds until the piece is almost finished, so you can't set up a patch list before you start. And there's little point in setting up a patch list after the work is done!

A useful compromise is to select a range of sounds which you want to work with, store them in the first few banks or program positions and then set up a partial patch list with them in. If you add new sounds, it's easy to add them to the end of the current selection and to insert them in the patch list.

❑ Setting up with Sys Ex

While you're working on a song, all your instruments have the sounds you need, the correct effects settings and so on. But once you start a new one these often get forgotten or abandoned.

On completion of a project, perform a Sys Ex bulk dump from all your instruments and store them on the same disk or in the same folder as the song data. Store each dump separately. If you need to go back to the song all the sounds will be there for you.

❑ Using an initialisation sequence

Before you play virtually any MIDI file you have to make various adjustments to the equipment – select suitable sounds, set the pitch bend range, adjust volume levels and so on. Most of this can be done via MIDI itself by including the relevant commands in a MIDI file. This can include a bulk dump of sounds as above but it can be a simpler setup routine such as initialising a GM or GS module. If you are creating GM files to give to others some sort of initialisation routine is essential to ensure that the music has a 'clean slate' to play on.

Unless you are bulk dumping voices, most initialisation sequences will not be very long. It's a good idea – and increasingly common practice on behalf of MIDI file programmers – to start a song at bar two or three and leave the first bar(s) for initialisation instructions.

If you have a separate initialisation message for each channel, you can put them on separate tracks (this is easiest done with pattern-based sequencers). Alternatively, you can put everything in one pattern and put it on one track but make sure the track parameters allow transmission on all MIDI channels.

You can create separate initialisation routines for different instruments and load them before you start work on a new piece. There's more about creating initialisation sequences in the following sections.

❑ Basic Sys Ex info

This isn't the place for a Sys Ex tutorial but here's a few basics. Like all MIDI data, Sys Ex data consists of a string of numbers or bytes as they are called. A byte can take a value from 0 to 127. The first few bytes of a Sys Ex message provide the following information:

Byte 1:   System Exclusive header

Byte 2: Manufacturer's identification
Byte 3: Device identification code
Byte 4: Device Number
Byte 5: Number of bytes in the data
Byte 6: First data byte...
The final two bytes hold the following information:
Penultimate Byte: Checksum value
Last Byte: End of System Exclusive byte

The bytes to indicate the start and end of a Sys Ex message are the same in all Sys Ex messages and are F0 and F7 respectively. This is hexadecimal notation, a nuisance to normal folk but very handy when working with computers. There's a decimal to hex conversion table in the Appendix to this book.

Most sequencers support Sys Ex messages (although some budget and early programs ignore it completely). If you load a Sys Ex message you should be able to see it in the Event editor. It may appear in hex or decimal and possibly show an ASCII translation. ASCII stands for the American Standard Code for Information Interchange and it's simply a set of numeric codes used for representing letters of the alphabet.

The ASCII translation probably won't make much sense although if you examine a bulk dump you may spot the names of sounds. You will almost certainly see the name of the instrument manufacturer which the sequencer gets from the second byte.

You can edit the data by inserting or changing the numbers. However, make sure you know what you're doing or you may alter parameters. A list of Sys Ex messages is usually given in the MIDI Data Format section of an instrument's manual.

☑ PROJECT

Entering a Sys Ex message

Most sequencer users are quite happy to hack about in the event editor altering notes and velocities, but many perceive Sys Ex messages as altogether more mysterious and complex.

Well, potentially more complex they may be, but that's only because they can carry a vast amount of data. Mysterious they are not. However, many sequencers handle Sys Ex in a slightly different way to notes so this can add to the confusion.

The first thing to do is read your sequencer's manual and see how it handles Sys Ex. Cubase, for example, puts a Sys Ex entry in the Event Type column of the List editor. Double click on the Comments entry and a Sys Ex editor line will appear. It uses Hexadecimal notation (see

Appendix for the conversion table) and you can clearly see all the instructions but it doesn't offer an ASCII translation.

A GS initialisation message in Cubase's Sys Ex editor.

Notator Logic's Event List has two Sys Ex filter buttons. One removes Sys Ex messages from the list completely, the other shows only the header but filters out the data. This is very useful as it lets you see that there's a Sys Ex message there but it spares you from several pages of data in the case of long voice dump data and the like.

Logic Sys Ex data is in decimal, not hex, and it does not actually show the first or last bytes – these are implied – but it does offer an ASCII translation.

The same GS initialisation message as it appears in Logic.

Let's enter a very simple Sys Ex message, a GM initialisation command which puts a GM unit into GM mode and sets all the parameters to their default values. This is the full message in hex and decimal:

Hex: F0, 7E, 7F, 9, 1, F7
Dec: 240, 126, 127, 9, 1, 247

1) Enter your sequencer's event list. You may have to create a track and/or a pattern first.

2) If the editor has an event filter, make sure Sys Ex messages are not filtered out of the display.

3) Insert a Sys Ex event. This may involve dragging a Sys Ex icon into the editor or clicking on a Sys Ex insert box.

4) If the editor has a Sys Ex data (not message) filter, switch this off so you can see all the data bytes.

5) If the sequencer has a special Sys Ex editor such as Cubase, simply type in the numbers. You'll probably have to separate them with commas – check the manual.

If you have to edit the numbers in the editor with the mouse, click and scroll to the required values. Make sure the message is the right length. For example, you increase and decrease the number of data bytes in Logic by clicking on the left or right chevrons bracketing the EOX (end of Sys Ex) entry. You can't simply set unwanted bytes to 0 and this will give the message a totally different meaning.

The GM initialisation message as it appears in Notator.

Check if your sequencer shows the start and end bytes. Don't try to enter them if it doesn't! The chances are you won't be able to do so anyway, as they are over 127.

That's it! Play this to a GM module and it will reset. Other Sys Ex messages can be entered in the same way.

☑ *PROJECT*

Checking the manufacturer's Sys Ex ID

If your sequencer shows an ASCII translation of Sys Ex data, change or scroll through the first data byte and you will see which identification numbers have been assigned to various manufacturers. These translations are built into most sequencers.

❏ The timing of Sys Ex data

Individual data bytes in Sys Ex messages do not have a time position of their own. The bars:beats:ticks position is that of the Sys Ex header. All the other bytes follow one after the other as quickly as possible.

When a Sys Ex message is being transmitted, no other event can be transmitted (except System Realtime events which keep time), so if you send a large Sys Ex message in the middle of a sequence there may be a hiccup. The overall timing of the song is maintained, it's just the notes which may be delayed.

☑ *PROJECT*

Setting up GM and GS files using Sys Ex

If you are creating a file to be played on a GM or GS instrument, insert a Sys Ex initialisation command at the start of the file to ensure the music begins with a clean slate. Failure to do so could cause unexpected results during playback if changes have previously been made to the module's default settings.

Hands On MIDI Software has a standard set of Sys Ex messages which are used at the start of all the company's files. They are reproduced here with kind permission. Create a separate pattern for each of the following Sys Ex messages. You can then select the ones you want and put them at the beginning of a song.

GM Initialisation. This puts a unit into GM mode and sets all its parameters to their default values.

F0, 7E, 7F, 09, 01, F7

GS Initialisation. This puts a unit into GS mode and sets all its parameters to their default values.

F0, 41, 10, 42, 12, 40, 00, 7F,00, 41, F7

Set Partial Reserve on a GS instrument
F0, 41, 10, 42, 12, 40, 01, 10,
02, 00, 01, 03, 02, 02, 02, 02, 02, 02, 01, 01, 01, 01, 01, 01,

17, F7

This is all one message but it has been divided into three sections for easy reference. The first line is the Partial Reserve command, the second line is the number of partials reserved for each part and the third line contains a checksum and the end of Sys Ex message.

The parts actually begin with the drum part so the first 02 in the second line reserves two partials for the drums. The second figure, 00, reserves no partials for part 1 as this is generally not used with GM/GS files. You can create your own partial reserve settings by altering the values in this line but note that they have to add up to 24.

Set Reverb to 90
F0, 41, 10, 42, 12, 40, 01, 33, 5A, 32, F7

Set Chorus to 90
F0, 41, 10, 42, 12, 40, 01, 3A, 5A, 2B, F7

If you don't like the idea of messing around with Sys Ex, Hands On has created a disk of GM/GS Sys Ex messages so you can select the ones you want and simply load them into your sequencer.

☑ PROJECT

Setting up GM and GS files using controllers

MIDI being what it is, some General MIDI units may not respond to Sys Ex messages as you might hope or expect. Hands On adopts a belt and braces approach and also uses a set of Controller messages to initialise a GM/GS sequence. These are as follows:

Position	Status	Chn	1st	2nd	Description
2:1:0	Control	1	120	0	All sound off
2:1:4	Control	1	121	0	Reset all Controllers
2:1:8	Control	1	1	0	Centre Mod wheel
2:1:12	Pitch Bend	1	64	0	Centre Pitch Bend
2:1:16	Control	1	7	100	Set Volume to 100
2:1:20	Control	1	11	127	Set Expression to full
2:1:24	Control	1	10	64	Set Pan to midway
2:1:28	Control	1	91	XX	Reverb
2:1:32	Control	1	93	YY	Chorus
2:1:36	Control	1	101	0	RPN MSB
2:1:40	Control	1	100	0	RPN LSB
2:1:44	Control	1	6	12	Pitch range to 1 octave
2:1:48	Control	1	101	127	RPN MSB
2:1:52	Control	1	100	127	RPN LSB

Some explanations may be in order. The position is the position of the controller messages in a sequence in bars:beats:ticks format. Using a resolution of 384 ppqn (pulses per quarter note) which many modern sequencers support, the events are 4 ticks apart. At a lower resolution of 96ppqn (very few sequencers have a lower resolution) the events will still be 1 tick apart. This ensures that all the messages are transmitted without getting in each other's way. If you have a sequencer with a lower resolution, or if some messages don't seem to be transmitting, just space them out more.

The status, chn, 1st and 2nd parameters are the settings and values to enter into your sequencer's Event editor. Insert your own XX and YY values to set the reverb and chorus levels respectively.

The next three instructions set the pitch bend to a one-octave range using registered parameter numbers (RPN). The final two instructions lock this so inadvertent twiddling of the data entry slider, for example, will not change the setting. A full description of RPNs is beyond the scope of this book but basically they allow the user to access sound parameters within an instrument, in this case, to set the pitch bend range.

LSB and MSB stand for least significant byte and most significant byte respectively and are used to supply values greater than 127 to a system in two chunks. Because of the way computer and MIDI numbering systems work, the maximum value a single parameter can have is 127. The MSB supplies values above this. All the above data should be inserted in your initialisation sequence 16 times, once for each MIDI channel. Change the chn value accordingly.

❑ Maximising GM's polyphony

Most GM units are 24- or 28-voice polyphonic (see *Not enough polyphony'* in Chapter 17 for more info about voices), and problems can occur if you exceed this. If polyphony – or lack of it – is a problem, there are two things you can do to help alleviate the situation.

1) Use Partial Reserve instructions to reserve a minimum number of voices for the most important parts. See *Setting up GM and GS files using Sys Ex*, a few entries earlier.

2) Use MIDI channels with a higher note priority rating for the most important parts. Most GM/GS units give priority to notes arriving on certain MIDI channels. Channel 10, the drum channel, gets highest priority which helps ensure that your drum track doesn't disappear. Then the priority runs through the channels from 1 to 16. So, assign your most important parts to the lowest numbered channels.

❑ Create your own riff library

As you work, you will probably build up a collection of useful drum and bass patterns and instrumental riffs. If you save these individually as patterns you will have a ready source of musical building blocks to draw on when creating new pieces.

If your sequencer does not let you save individual patterns check if it lets you merge a MIDI file with an existing file. If it does, save patterns as standard MIDI files.

However, if you have many patterns it can be time consuming to load them one at a time. To speed up the selection process, save similar types of patterns in one file.

❑ Undo/redo flips

Undo and redo functions let you quickly flip between two edits and can be used to perform an A/B comparison to see which one you prefer. For example, put the section music you want to edit into a loop, perform the edit and use undo and redo to switch between the original and the edited version.

❑ Channel filters

Many sequencers have a channel filter which lets you specify MIDI channels which will not be recorded. Use this when recording a performance from another sequencer or workstation if you don't want all the parts. You may, for example, decide you only want the drums on channel 10 and the bass line on 2.

Of course, you could simply record everything and delete the unwanted bits later. However, the less data you record the more accurate the timing will be (see the 'Files' section for more on file transfers). Also, if your computer is short of memory, it makes sense to omit the parts you don't want.

❑ Using editor filters

When using an editor such as an event list which can show several different types of event at the same time, the events that you want to edit can sometimes get lost among the other events. Controller data is the worst culprit as there is usually so much of it. Many sequencers have a display filter which removes unwanted events from the editor's display (it doesn't delete them) enabling you to concentrate on the ones you want.

Under normal circumstances you won't need to see Sys Ex events. Some editors show note off events which are generally not very helpful.

Most editors, however, also show the length of the notes and this is far easier to comprehend and edit.

❑ Punching in

Punching in and out of a track is a throwback to the days of analogue multi-track tape machines when it was the only way to record over an error. With modern sequencers this is no longer the case as you can edit the offending notes in many ways. If you've come to sequencing from audio recording, you may still be tempted to use punch in but it is now really redundant.

So, don't punch in. It's far easier and safer to re-record a section. Mute or cut the offending part and then merge it with the new bit.

❑ To edit or re-record?

It's often easier and quicker to re-record a part than it is to edit it unless the error is only a couple of notes. Don't edit just because you have the tools.

❑ The benefits of cycling

Cycle or loop mode is useful if you want to practise a part to go with music you have already recorded. You can set the loop going and jam over it until you come up with a new music line.

Use it, too, when setting up parameters such as patch, volume, velocity, transpose, pan and so on so you can hear the changes immediately without having to start and stop the sequencer.

❑ Overdub recording

Many sequencers have an overdub mode which merges a new recording with existing data. If you go into cycle mode you can loop around a few bars of music adding new parts to it on each pass.

Many musicians like working this way as it doesn't disturb the creative juices. It's commonly used to create drum parts, adding a new drum sound on each pass. This also helps give a human feel to the pattern.

However, it's sometimes useful to be able to edit individual drum lines. If your sequencer has a drum editor or an extract by note function which you can apply to the drum track you may still be able to this. But having said all that, some sequencers let you change tracks during cycle record mode and some will even increment tracks automatically after each loop. These give you the benefits of cycle recording without the disadvantages.

4 Ghost tracks

Many sequencers let you create ghost tracks, parts which 'borrow' note information from another track. The data is not actually duplicated as in a copy process which means it is very economical of memory.

But the main advantage of a ghost track is that if you change the notes in the original track, the ghosts will automatically use those notes, too. However, ghost tracks can still have their own set of attributes such as transpose, delay and so on. They can be used to create a wide range of effects. See also the sections on delays and transposition.

❑ No ghost facility?

If your sequencer lacks a ghost facility, you can still create all the ghost effects mentioned here by the 'older' method of physically copying tracks. Obviously, if you change the original part you will have to copy it to all the 'ghosts', too.

❑ Easy riffs

If you are recording a song which contains repetitive sections such as bass lines or chord progressions, instead of recording each repetition individually or even creating physical copies, use ghost tracks. You can then easily change all the riffs by changing the master one.

Name	Patch	Prog				
Track 1	GM Acou Grand Piano	0				
Track 2	GM Elec Grand Piano	2				
Track 3	GM Cello	42				
Track 4		OFF				
Track 5		OFF				

Track - BLUES1.SNG — Pattern Snap | Bar | Multitrack Recording | Off

Procyon displays ghost patterns, which it calls children, with a dotted outline. You can see the four original patterns which have been 'ghosted' to make a 12-bar blues.

☑ *PROJECT*

Layers on layers

Most sequencers can only transmit a track on one MIDI channel at a time. Ghost – and copied – tracks, therefore, are very useful for creating layered sounds. Here are some suggestions for layers, combinations of voices which sound good together. Try each of them on a variety of material and see which combinations sound best with your songs.

If you have a piano line, add a hint of another percussion sound such as vibes or harp.

Piano layered with strings is a very old but effective combination. Ideal for smoochy songs and romantic instrumental solos.

Use strings, vocal sounds and sweeps to build up a complex layered pad.

Layer a very short percussive sound with a longer one such as choirs, strings or a pad to create a dual sound which starts strongly but finishes more gently.

If one of the sounds in a layer has a slow attack, it will only come to the fore on long notes. This can be used very effectively with a piano/string layer.

5 | *Handling controllers*

❏ Controlling your controllers

You don't have to record the pitch bend or mod wheel while you're playing the keyboard – you can record it afterwards. In fact, it's a good idea to record it onto a separate track. It's easier to edit if it's not mixed in with note data and you can record several 'takes' on different tracks without recording the notes again.

❏ Thinning memory eaters

If a song contains a lot of pitch bend, mod wheel or continuous controller data, it could clog up the MIDI data stream and cause timing problems. This sort of data also takes up a considerable amount of memory.

Continuous controller data is often recorded with a higher precision than is needed as the ear is far less sensitive to these sort of changes than it is to pitch, for example. You can usually remove some of the data without changing the way we hear the music.

Procyon Pro lets you selectively remove one continuous event in every so-many so you can monitor the effect of gradually reducing the amount of data.

If you think continuous controller data is causing a problem, check if your sequencer has a Thin Controller or Reduce Controller function – but do save your work first. You can save memory and reduce the amount of data being thrown out the MIDI port.

❑ Roll your own controllers

Some sequencers have graphic data edit screens and these are very useful for creating data which your instruments may not be able to generate. If your keyboard doesn't have a pitch bend or modulation wheel – draw the data in.

Some sequencers have a Transform function which can convert one type of MIDI data into another. Use this to convert pitch bend into modulation data, for example (although a degree of imagination is required here). You could also use either of these wheels to generate data to control volume or tempo

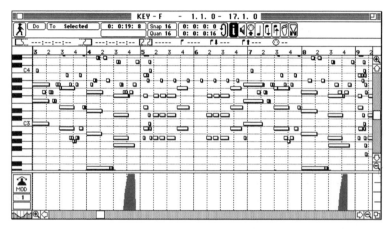

The graphic controller editor below the Edit screen in Cubase where you can insert and edit any type of controller data.

6 *Quantisation*

One of the major benefits and attractions of a sequencer is the quantise function which pulls errant notes into line with the beat. One of the most vexed questions in sequencing is whether to quantise or not.

☑ PROJECT

Partial quantisation

Unless you require absolute precision, always use partial quantisation. This is usually set as a percentage. For example, a setting of 75% will pull the notes 75% of the way towards the beat they should be on. Partial quantisation preserves some human timing inaccuracies which make music sound interesting while still helping to correct poor timing.

Record a music line and apply various degrees of quantisation to it. See how little you can apply in order to pull the notes into line without removing the human feel from it altogether.

Quantize	
Quantize Setting	16 ⬓
Percentage Change	05
Scope	
From C -2 **To** G 8	
○ **All** ◉ **Range**	
OK	**Cancel**

Procyon Pro lets you specify a partial quantise setting as a percentage.

❑ Dance music

Many people who criticise music produced with the aid of a sequencer claim it is mechanical and robotic. But this effect is exactly what is required by many forms of modern dance music so where metronomic precision is required, use a percentage setting of 100, particularly in the drum, bass and rhythm sections of the song.

❑ Humanising dance music

Notwithstanding the previous tip, even sections of modern dance music can benefit from a little 'human error'. This is more commonly called 'feel'. Unless you specifically want a heavily quantised effect, use smaller percentages in the lead lines and other parts which don't drive the beat in order to retain a degree of feel. You may be surprised how little you actually need quantise a music line to correct its timing.

❑ Quantising classical music

Classical music is very precise. Most of it is intended to be performed 'as written' with little scope for variations in timing. If all the members of a 64-piece orchestra did their own thing the music would be well out of step.

So generally, classical music consisting of many instrument parts can be quantised quite heavily. However, still with the aim of maintaining some sort of human input, try various degrees of partial quantisation before whacking it up to 100%.

❑ Random quantisation

We're going to get philosophical. Many sequencers have a Randomisation function which can be applied to various parameters such as velocity and note lengths and start times. If you have recorded a piece in step-time, you may think that a little randomisation might give it a human touch. It might.

The problem is, random to a computer is exactly that. The randomness introduced when we play with 'feeling' is much more considered and orderly than random numbers.

So beware how you use randomisation otherwise the music will sound like the product of a disordered mind rather than a musical one. The bottom line is this – it's probably better to add a little randomisation to a step-time entry than to leave it fully quantised but ultimately, your ears must be the jury. Your listeners will be the judge.

❑ Feeling groovy

A far better way to humanise a part is to use grooves. These are quantisation templates based on certain rhythm structures or derived from the feel of live recordings. Some sequencers let you create your own grooves and load new grooves from disk which opens the market for third-party groove designers.

Grooves were originally intended to let users apply a particular type of rhythmic feel such as swings, shuffles and pushes to a part.

You can design your own grooves in Cubase.

They are, of course, excellent for this. If you've recorded a pretty funky bass line, use it to create a groove template and apply it to other rhythmic parts of the song to make sure they 'groove' together.

If you want to humanise a part which has been recorded in step-time, create or use a groove based on a similar section of music. But note the difference between quantisation and grooves. Quantisation corrects timing errors. Grooves may do so but are primarily designed to apply a rhythmic feel to a pattern.

✓ PROJECT

Grooving straight beats

A groove can seriously alter the feel of a music line. You've recorded a bass line or chord part which doesn't quite feel right – throw it a few grooves and see what happens.

Grooves such as swing can be amazingly effective on certain types of classical music. They can transform it without destroying the harmony or structure. Bach is a great candidate for all sorts of musical manipulations. Record some Bach (many MIDI file companies have Bach MIDI files) and throw it a few grooves. Sacrilegious? Possibly, but how do you think Jacques Loussier started?

Tempo tricks

There are no MIDI messages for tempo changes as such but most sequencers have their own Tempo Pseudo Event or a Conductor or Tempo track in which tempos appear in a list a little like an event editor or else appear graphically on a grid.

❏ Recording tempo changes
If you are recording a piece of music which you want to contain changes of tempo, record it all at one tempo and insert the tempo changes afterwards. This keeps the note/bar relationship intact and, providing you can mute the tempo track, it makes it easier to add other parts.

Procyon Pro has a graphic Tempo Conductor track which makes it easy to see where tempo changes occur.

❏ Rallentandos and accelerandos
You can create gradual tempo changes manually by inserting tempo change instructions at various points throughout the piece. However, several sequencers have a Tempo Scale function which lets you program a start and an end tempo across a specified range of bars. It will then automatically insert the required tempo changes. Some even let you select logarithmic or linear progressions. Even so, these may not produce exactly the result you're after so be prepared for a little editing.

❏ No tempo scaling?

If your sequencer doesn't have tempo scaling, you'll have to insert tempo changes by hand and this could require some experimentation. Smooth changes may require two or more new tempos per bar. However, as with controller data (we tend to record far more controller changes that the ear can discern), you can usually produce very effective tempo changes with remarkable little data.

```
┌─────────────────────────────────────────┐
│          Change Conductor                │
│  ─────────────────────────────────────   │
│   From Measure  16  to  32               │
│                      4                   │
│  ☐ Set Meter to  ─── and Beat to  ♩ ▲    │
│                      4                    ▼│
│  ○ Set all Tempos to  120                │
│  ○ Change to  100  % of current values   │
│  ◉ Change smoothly from  100  to  120    │
│  ○ Change smoothly from  100 % to 100 %  │
│  ○ Add  0   to all values                │
│  ☐ Limit low values to  10               │
│  ☐ Limit high values to  300             │
│  ( Cancel )              (   OK   )       │
└─────────────────────────────────────────┘
```

Mastertracks Pro will automatically produce scaled tempo changes.

❏ A track of its own

If your sequencer supports tempo events but doesn't have a conductor track, reserve a track especially for them. They'll be far easier to edit if the track isn't encumbered by note data and if you want to run the piece at one tempo, say to record additional material, you can mute the track.

8 Transposition

Most sequencers have a transpose function which you can usually apply to individual tracks or even to a range of selected events. The most obvious use of transposition is to change the key of a song but it has far more interesting and subtle uses, too.

❏ Defeating transposition

Before you start transposing, have you any drum tracks? If so, you won't want to transpose them otherwise the drums will be playing on another kit altogether! Many sequencers let you specify certain MIDI channels or tracks which will not be affected by the transpose function. This may be called Transpose Off or Disable Transpose. Use this to preserve your drums.

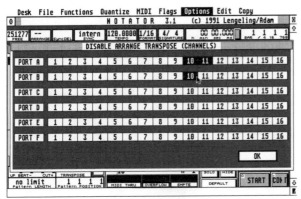

The Disable Transpose function in Notator lets you protect selected MIDI channels from transposition.

❏ Beefier bass lines

This may seem obvious but try transposing a bass line down an octave. Some synths, particularly GM sound modules, don't always have the bass sounds as low as they might be. Use a deep synth bass sound with lots of harmonics for an analogue effect.

❑ Doubling up

Transpose can be used in many creative ways with ghost tracks. Double up on a sound by transposing a ghost track up or down by an octave. This can sound great on piano parts – as if a real virtuoso is playing. Don't be content with transposing by an octave. Try transposing by two octaves. This really spreads out the music line.

Octaves work best with monophonic parts such as melodies. The result is muddy if you transpose clusters of chords. Octaves work particularly well with piano, organ and stab brass sounds. Under certain circumstances it can also work with bass lines although you must exercise discretion with the bass sounds you choose and you must be careful that the transposed part does not move outside the bass range.

☑ PROJECT

Instant harmonies 1

You can use Transpose to produce quick harmony lines although there is a caveat. Transpose functions usually work in semitone increments and these do not produce perfect harmonies on all degrees of the scale.

Try the following examples so you can hear what sort of results are possible. Record a scale of C on one track and copy it to another track which you can transpose. Let's say you want to create a line a third below it like this:

Transpose the second track down by three semitones and it will look like this:

Five out of eight of the transposed notes are at the pitch we want them. Listen to the result. Now transpose it down by four semitones like this:

Only three of the notes are right.

The first example is actually a parallel scale in A and the second is a parallel scale in Ab. The 'safest' transpositions, that is the ones which come closest to a perfect harmony, are five and seven semitones. Try those and see which sound the best.

You could, of course, alter the offending notes by hand but your sequencer may be able to do it for you. What you need is a search and replace function. Some sequencers actually have this feature but on most it lurks behind a Transform function. The exact process you use will depend on how this works.

If you can selectively transpose specific notes, select the offending ones and transpose them. Alternatively, you may have to physically convert them into another note rather than transpose them. Make sure you catch notes in all octaves.

There, that wasn't too difficult. It's easier than recording the harmony line separately and it ensures that the timing of the two lines is exactly the same.

Transpositions of a third, fourth and fifth are particularly effective with vocal sounds.

❑ Instant harmonies 2

Some enlightened sequencers such as Cubase actually have a Scale Correction feature which changes transposed notes to the key of the source track. Saves an awful lot of work. Check your manual.

❑ Alternative harmonies

Cubase also has a fascinating device called the IPS – Interactive Phrase Synthesiser. It's far too complex to go into here but it's well worth working your way through it on a wet afternoon. One of the things it

Interactive Phrase Synthesizer

Phrase Input
Phrase   **Empty**
8. 0 **1** **0**
Length   Notes Numbers

Interpreter
Mode   **Transp. Ret.**
Hold **Loop** **Retrig** **S**

MIDI Input
Sort   **Highest Note**
Thru **C-2** to **68**

Dynamics
Off   **0**
LFO Freq **100**   Add/Sub

Pitch
ON   **Major**   **C**
Correct   to scale   in key
Off   **0**
LFO Freq **100** Dens **1000** Trans

Rhythm
Off   **100** **Off** **Off**
LFO Freq **100** Comp% Len Q

Functions
Active   **Init**

Output
Modem
Prg **1** Chan **1**

Global
Combi   **Store**
Empty
Thru Program **No**

Modulator 1
Dest **Midi-Out-Channel** **0**
Min
Off   **Off**
LFO Freq **100** Ampl **1000** Q

Modulator 2
Dest **Midi-Out-Channel** **1**
Min
Off   **Off**
LFO Freq **100** Ampl **1000** Q

IPS A **ON**
0. 0

IPS B **ON**
0. 0

Cubase's IPS is well worth spending a wet afternoon with.

can do is change the scale or tonality of a piece. There are 20 built-in scales such as Hungarian, Japanese, Persian, Blues and so on and these can dramatically affect the character of a tune.

❑ Over the top harmonies

Instead of creating a harmony note below the melody note, create one above it but reduce its volume so it's not as loud as the melody note. An interval of a third, fourth or fifth above can produce an interesting Country & Western effect.

☑ *PROJECT*

Instant harmonies 3

Here are some harmony suggestions intended mainly for sequencers with a scale correction feature. You can produce these effects without one but they will entail a little more work.

Chords1: create two harmony voices such as a fifth and an octave for a fuller sound.
Chords2: use intervals based on major or minor chords.
Chords3: Add a third, fifth and a sixth for a close harmony jazz sound.
Chords4: add a ninth to one of the above harmonies.
Chords5: create a spread chord containing four or five notes over a two-octave span.

☑ *PROJECT*

More colourful harmonies

As each harmony has been generated on a different track, it's an easy matter to assign a different sound to each one. This can be used very effectively with brass chords, for example, vocal parts or a woodwind section. The variations in tone add a new dimension to the chord.

❑ Instant chords

Emagic's Logic sequencer has a Chord Memorizer which allows an incoming note to play a chord of up to twelve notes, all of which can be on different MIDI devices. This enables you to create a custom chord for each note and to select different sounds for them, too.

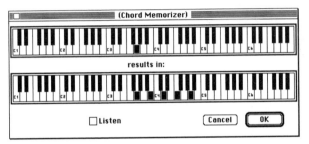

Create your own chords from single notes with Logic.

❑ Keep on strumming 1

If you have created a harmony consisting of notes on several tracks, delay the tracks to produce a strum effect.

Delaying tracks in Cubase to produce a strum effect.

❑ Keep on strumming 2

Logic has an Arpeggiator in its Environment page which can create strums and arpeggios for you.

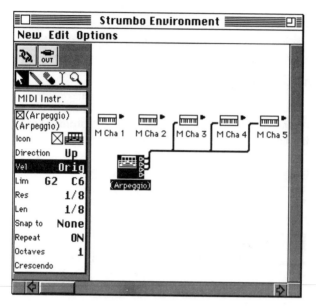

Creating arpeggios in Notator Logic.

❑ Classic chorus booster

Give your song a lift by transposing the last chorus upwards by a tone or a semitone. Barry Manilow's *Can't Smile Without You* contains several semitone transpositions throughout the song.

Delaying tactics

Most sequencers have a delay or track offset facility which lets you shift a track backwards or forwards a little in relation to the other tracks. The delay time may be given in clock ticks or note durations. This has several uses.

❏ Slow lines

If you are using a sound such as strings with a slow attack, it may appear to be entering a little later than you would like. To correct this, shift the track back in time a little so it starts to play sooner than the others.

❏ MIDI Echo – general info

You can use delays to create MIDI echoes. Create one ghost track for each echo you require. It's very easy to produce three or four echoes. One thing to be aware of is that each echo will use one note's worth of polyphony. You may get away with this if the sound or notes are very short.

MIDI echoes have several advantages over echoes produced by FX units. It's easy to regulate the timing to fit the tempo of a song. As MIDI echoes are programmed into the sequencer and defined as a division of a beat, if you alter the tempo, the echo changes, too. Not so easy to do with an FX unit.

Also, you are creating first-generation sounds so the signal will be cleaner than one coming from an FX unit. And it frees up your FX unit for other things.

☑ PROJECT

Echo timing

Create a music line and test the effect of various MIDI echoes. Try delaying echo tracks in increments of the beat – by 1/16th notes, for example. Also, try using values in between the beat. If a line uses 1/8th notes, try a 1/16th note delay.

If you have to enter delay times in ticks, you need to know the timing resolution or timebase of your sequencer. Assuming a timebase of 192 (which means there are 192 clock ticks per quarter note), these are the values for the following note durations:

1/4 note:	192
1/8 note:	96
1/16 note:	48
1/32 note:	24
1/64 note:	12

☑ *PROJECT*

Echo volume

After creating some MIDI echoes as described above, try adjusting their volume. One of the attributes of natural echoes is that they die away. To mimic this, reduce the volume or velocity of each successive echo. You may be able to do this using MIDI volume although most sequencers give you more control over velocity than volume by allowing you to add or subtract a velocity offset to a track.

Using velocity has its own benefits and advantages. If you prefer to control the volume use expression if you can rather than volume. See the section *More Expressive Music* (Chapter 11) for more information about this.

❏ Slapback echo

You can thicken a sound by adding a very short echo, somewhat less than a 1/32nd note. This is the equivalent of an FX unit's doubling or slapback echo setting.

☑ *PROJECT*

Multi-sound echoes

One fascinating option well worth exploring is to give each echo a different sound – you can't do that with an FX unit. If the echoes are on different tracks, simply set them to transmit on a different MIDI channel and select a sound accordingly. Try a vibes echo on a piano line or a vocal chorus echo on strings.

❏ Transposing echoes

Try transposing the echoes. Octaves often work best but try thirds, fourths and fifths, too. Check out the *Transposition* section for more transposition ideas.

☑ *PROJECT*

Panning echoes

Another useful ploy is to pan the echoes. If the main line is in the centre of the stereo spread, pan the first echo hard left and the second one hard right.

This is incredibly effective, particularly with sounds which have a percussive edge. Variations on this theme include creating a series of four or more echoes which pan from left to right.

❑ **Multi sound/pitch/pan echoes**

Put several ideas together and create transposed echoes, panned and using different sounds! You can build up an incredibly complex sound all from a single note.

❑ **Echoes and drums**

You can also create interesting effects by applying echoes to drum tracks. You probably wouldn't want to echo a whole drum track but a slap-back echo on selected snare beats or ethnic percussion sounds can be very effective.

☑ *PROJECT*

Pre-echo

A variation on the echo idea is the pre-echo – an echo which comes BEFORE the sound! Instead of delaying the echo track, bring it forward.

You may have to take a little more care selecting the echo sound and its volume/velocity otherwise the pre-echo will pre-empt the main line. Aim to create a subtle hint or suggestion of a sound. This works best with slow lines.

10 Drum pattern programming

Drum programming is an art in itself and there are as many ways of recording a drum track as there are musicians.

One of the most common ways is the drum machine method which involves creating one or two-bar drum patterns and chaining them together to form a finished song. Some sequencers have a dedicated drum pattern editor which can be a great help if you use this method. Other sequencers have a graphic editor which lets you draw events onto a grid. Useful for 'drawing in' hi hats, for example.

An alternative is to use a dedicated drum pattern editor such as Drumatix (Newtronic) for the ST and PC or PC Drummer (PC Services) and export the result into your main sequencer.

If you don't use a drum editor, it's a good idea to keep each drum on a separate track. They're much easier to edit that way and you can always combine them into one drum track later on.

When you're reading through these tips, if in doubt always err on the side of subtlety.

❏ Setting up a drum editor

Drum editors generally show a list of drums on the left against a pattern grid on the right. They can typically handle 60 drums or more and scrolling through the list each time to find a hi tom is not conducive to creative programming.

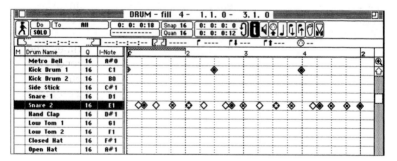

You can rearrange the drums in Cubase by dragging them up and down the list.

Few drum patterns use more than a dozen different sounds so before you start, move the drums which form the heart of your pattern to the top of the list. You may also want to put all the toms together, for example. Optimising the list in this way will let you work far more efficiently.

☑ PROJECT

Avoiding the machine gun effect

But putting the right drum sounds at the right place in a pattern is only part of the process. Patterns recorded in step-time can turn out to be a little lifeless and mechanical. For example, does your sixteenth-note hi hat line sound like a machine gun? If so, all the notes probably have the same velocity. Most drum editors give you a couple of tools for entering hits at different velocities.

Create a basic rock pattern with 1/16th note hi hats all at the same velocity. Now vary the velocities. Make those on beats two and four slightly louder. Does that sound better?

❏ Randomisation?

A popular way to humanise drum tracks is to sprinkle a bit of randomisation around. You can apply this to the velocities and the start times of the notes.

However, randomisation is not the panacea it may at first appear to be. Sure, a drummer never hits two drums at exactly the same time or with the same force but the velocity and start times vary in a musical way, not a random way – at least not if the drummer knows his stuff.

So, a reasonable plan of action might be to accent the notes on the beat and then apply a smidgen of randomisation. Some sequencers allow you to select notes for editing which fall within certain divisions of the beat so you may be able to select just the notes in a track which fall on beats one and three, for example.

You could also add a little randomisation to the start times. The secret, as with most things in life, is moderation. The differences we are looking to create should be noticeable on a subconscious or musical level rather than a conscious one. If you listen to a drum part and can hear the randomness, you've overdone it.

❏ Multiple drums and hi hats

Another trick to beef up your drum patterns is to use two or more different drum sounds to add timbral variation. A drum will sound different depending not only on how hard but where you hit it.

With a sampler, it's usually fairly easy to introduce a timbral variation which is tied to velocity. Make a higher velocity produce a slightly higher pitch. It's easy, too, to detune a drum a little and assign it to another MIDI note. Use the two drum sounds instead of the one.

Most synthesisers also allow a degree of control over drum sounds in the way of tuning and modulation and these can be used in the same way.

If you have a fixed set of drum sounds, check if they respond to pitch bend. If so, add a dash of pitch bend to some drum hits. It's probably easiest to draw this into a graphic controller editor although you could use an event list. You'll need to select the drums carefully, however, as pitch bend will affect all sounds on the drum channel.

❏ Hitting your drum and bending it

To avoid the previous problem, set up two MIDI channels for drums – one for normal drums and one you can use with pitch bend.

This can actually be useful if you are interested in ethnic percussion. Drums such as the Indian tabla have built-in pitch bend. If there's no tabla in your kit, try a tom tom or bongo and use pitch bend to bend the pitch up and down over the duration of the note.

Most GM/GS instruments can play a drum kit only on channel 10, so you will not be able to try this with them. You could, however, use the individual drum voices at the higher end of the program number range. Assign them to their own track and MIDI channel and bend them.

❏ Extraneous hits

Another ploy to make a drum track seem more human is to throw in additional drum hits throughout the song – a double bass drum hit here, an extra closed hi hat here. This avoids the feeling that the track was constructed from three patterns linked together. Even if it was.

❏ Triplet fills

Say your rhythm is in a rock-steady 4/4 and you want a fill to take you from one section to the next, don't automatically do 1/16th notes on the toms, try a triplets fill. This breaks up the pattern and can lead very nicely into the next section. In fill-type situations even on snare, try triplets instead of 1/8th or 1/16ths.

❏ Recording real-time drums

In spite of these tips, some people think you just can't get a good feel in step-time. You can give your drum tracks a more human feel by recording them in real-time. This has the advantage of retaining human timing and the chances are similar patterns in consecutive bars will not be exactly alike, further adding to the human feel. The disadvantage is that if you decide to change the format of the song it may not be so easy to cut out or paste in a few bars.

Many people, especially beginners, lay down the bass drum line first usually followed by the snare. However, you'll get a much better feel if you record these both at the same time, as in normal drum playing they are usually inexorably linked. Next you can add a hi hat line and then any other drum toppings you like.

❑ Tidy drum note lengths

You can use a very short note duration with drums and still have them play out in full because drum sounds are usually 'one shot' sounds. That is, once triggered they play in their entirety. They tend not to respond to note off messages. Real drums have no note off – unless the drummer puts his hand on the drum to mute it!

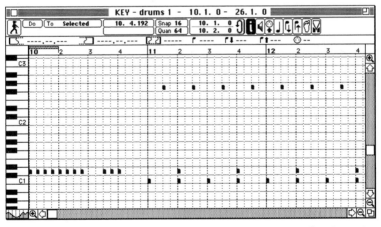

Using short note lengths for drums makes it easy to see where the notes are.

This being so, the actual duration of a drum note is usually not important and many MIDI file programmers use a short duration which may vary from 1 to 8 clock ticks. This looks tidy and you can easily alter the note durations using a global length change command.

❑ Note lengths and old drum machines

Some older drum units require drum notes to be a little longer than a few ticks. If you have reduced the length of the drum notes you are programming and they don't play properly on a particular instrument, try increasing their length.

❑ Buy a drummer

Not all great songwriters are great drummers. If Steve Gadd is busy this weekend and can't make your session, don't be afraid to use 'building block' files. You can load these into your sequencer and cut and paste them to fit your song.

❑ Instant arrangements

An even easier although less customisable way to create drum tracks and backing tracks quickly is to use a program such as Jammer (Et Cetera), Session Partner (Newtronic) or Band-In-A-Box (Arbiter). These will give you an instant groove and once you've done some work on your song you can go over the bits the program created. Or not.

❑ Drum tracks that groove

Many sequencers have a groove function which is a special type of quantise. Instead of shoving notes onto regular divisions of the beat, a groove will move them onto predetermined divisions. For example, some grooves have a swing setting. Apply this to a run of sixteenth notes, for example, and they will become dotted eighths followed by thirty-second notes - and swing. Other grooves may give a track a push or hold it back or turn it into triplets.

Grooves are well worth exploring it you're looking for a particular feel. Most sequencers with grooves come with several examples. You can usually create your own and more are often available for loading into the program. Of course, grooves aren't limited to use with drum tracks.

❑ A groove of your own

Some sequencers can read a track and create a groove from it. This enables you to apply a particular feel to other tracks. Take the groove from the drum track, for example, and apply it to the bass line.

❑ Driving the rhythm

Move a drum track forward so it starts earlier than the rest of the music. This will give the impression that the rhythm is driving the tune along. But don't move it too far otherwise it will sound out of sync.

File Edit Structure Functions Options Audio Windows Tools

	Over Quantize	
Snap	BAR	Mouse
	Note On Quantize	
A	M	C	Track	Chn	Inst
	Iterative Quantize	
	drums 1	10
	Analytic Quantize	

Menu items shown:

Over Quantize
Note On Quantize
Iterative Quantize
Analytic Quantize
Groove Quantize ▶

Undo Quantize
Freeze Quantize
Setup Quantize...

Logical ▶
Freeze Play Parameter
Legato
Length Size
Fixed Length
Delete Doubles
Delete Cont. Data
Reduce Cont. Data

Transpose/Velocity ... ⌘H

Groove submenu:
Straight
PushB2&4
LateB2&4
PushP234
LateP234
PushB1&3
8 Triplt
16Triplt
SOLO 3a4
ShflS2&4
ShflM2&4
ShflH2&4
Move ALL
PushFILL
LateFILL
DNA 32nd

Track list:
	drums 2	10
	perc	10
	bass	6
	Piano	8
	sequenz	3
	shore	7
	brass	2
	horns	9
	pad	15
	strings	14
	o.hit	12
	chor	13
	(vocal)	1

Cubase comes with several 'DNA' drum grooves.

❏ Lazy drummer

If you have recorded the drum parts on separate tracks, try moving just the snare forward a little to give the track a push. Alternatively, for a 'lazy' feel, push the snare back a little.

❏ Doubling up

Rhythm tracks can change quite dramatically if you double or half their speed without changing the tempo of the accompaniment. Some sequencers have a double and half tempo function which can do this.

❏ Exotic percussion

You can make even a standard rock pattern more interesting by including a smattering of exotic percussion sounds. The addition of an agogo or bongo hit every two or four bars can make a pattern more individual and outstanding.

❏ Alternative drum sounds

Drum hits do not have to come from a drum kit – you can also use percussion patches in your synth. If fact, you don't even have to use percussion sounds! Investigate other sounds which could punctuate a drum track. This could be anything from a filter-swept bass to a vocal aah sound.

More expressive music

Even with today's samplers and synthesisers which can mimic acoustic instrument sounds amazingly well, there is more to creating a realistic music part than simply getting the notes right. Here's a varied collection of ideas to help you create more realistic music lines and more expressive music.

❑ Expression vs. Volume

Controller 7 is Volume and Controller 11 is Expression. Both control the volume on a MIDI channel so which one do you use and when?

It may help to think of them in terms of the volume controls on an organ. There will be a master volume slider or knob, the equivalent of our Volume Controller 7. It will also have a volume pedal, commonly known as the expression pedal, which is used to adjust the volume while you play. This is, no doubt, where the term Expression came from.

Use Volume to set the overall level of a part and Expression to make any subsequent changes in volume to that part. Why? Well, say you use three dozen Volume messages to create a crescendo and later want to reduce the volume of the crescendo in relation to the other music parts. You'll have to change every one of the 36 Volume entries.

If you use Expression to create the crescendo, you can adjust its volume relative to the other parts with a single Volume instruction.

Also, if you give a file to someone else and they play it on a different instrument whose sounds are at different levels they can use Volume to tweak it to their instrument while still retaining any volume changes in the files which you have created with Expression.

❑ No Expression?

Unfortunately, not all instruments respond to Expression messages. You can tell if yours does by looking in the MIC (MIDI Implementation Chart), the section at the back of the manual which looks like a manic games of noughts and crosses. It'll be in the Control Change section and you want to see Controller 11. It will usually be named as Expression in the right hand column under Remarks.

If your instrument does support Expression but it doesn't seem to be working, check if you have to switch it on first from a parameter menu.

If your instrument doesn't support Expression, use Volume instead. It's not the most flexible solution but everyone used it before Expression caught on and it works.

❏ Expression/Volume vs. Velocity

The track parameters box in sequencers usually includes a Velocity parameter with which you can add or subtract an offset to the velocity of the data on a track. Many people use this to tweak the volume and in most cases it works fine.

However, velocity and volume are not the same. Sounds are often constructed so they change according to velocity. Brass sounds may have more 'rasp' while sounds which employ velocity switching may change altogether although these changes depend on the way the sounds have been programmed. You can probably find a brass sound in one of your instruments whose timbre changes with velocity. Usually, high velocity values produce a more raspy, harsher sound.

If a sound uses velocity to change its timbre, don't alter the velocity to make a volume change. For example, you may want a raspy brass sound but you may not want it very loud. In this case crank up the velocity and lower the volume.

Some sequencers have a Volume setting in the track parameters box as well as one for Velocity so use this or insert a Controller 7 instruction in the track and use this to adjust the volume.

Sounds in some instruments can distort when played at full velocity so it's a good idea to leave a little headroom.

❏ More feel

The timing resolution of sequencers typically ranges from 96 to 480ppqn (pulses per quarter note). 160 and 240 should be fine for most users but those with an acute sense of timing may occasionally wish for even greater timing accuracy particularly in slow pieces.

Timebase	
○ 48	◉ 192
○ 72	○ 224
○ 96	○ 240
○ 120	○ 384
○ 144	○ 480
○ 168	○ 720

Procyon Pro lets you choose from a large number of Timebase values.

Some sequencers, particularly those on the PC, let you change the timebase. This is primarily to compensate for slower machines. However, on any computer, you can double the timing resolution by doubling the tempo – it's as simple as that. But note that all duration and quantisation values will be half the normal value. For example, to quantise to an eight note, use a quarter note and so on.

❏ Better wind parts

Creating convincing orchestral instrument music lines isn't simply a matter of using the right sound – you have to play the line the way an instrumentalist would play it.

You can increase the authenticity of wind and brass parts by applying pitch bend at the beginning of notes so they rise up to the pitch. This is most easily done by drawing in pitch bend in a graphic editor. You can create several shades of bend and paste them onto the beginning of notes. Don't forget to leave spaces between phrases – wind players have to breathe, too!

❏ Pitch bend vibrato

It's very difficult for a brass player, for example, to maintain an even pitch on long notes and the sound will usually have a degree of vibrato. The vibrato applied to synthesised brass sounds in most instruments is generally too regular to be totally realistic although some instruments can add a degree of randomness to the vibrato which can improve matters.

You can create your own vibrato by adding very tiny degrees of pitch bend, nothing more than small spikes, throughout the duration of sustained brass notes. This will help simulate the wavering which occurs during playing. Again, these are best drawn in using a graphic controller editor.

❏ More mono realism

Most orchestral instruments of the wind and string family can only play one note at a time. If your sequencer has a Remove Overlaps function, use it to make monophonic lines more realistic. It can also be used on bass guitar lines, too.

❏ Smoothy

Some sequencers have a Make Legato function. This is not the opposite or reverse of Remove Overlaps. It extends the lengths of notes so there is no or very little gap between them so they play smoothly.

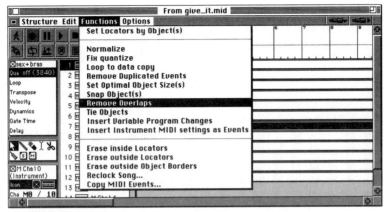

Logic's Remove Overlaps function can help create more realistic monophonic lines.

This is useful for smoothing out disjointed playing. You may have recorded a part using a sound with a little sustain so it wasn't necessary to hold down the key for the full duration of the note. It's also a style of playing popular in romantic piano solos.

Sometimes a full legato setting may be too much and the result may be too 'smooth'. Some sequencers let you set an amount by which the notes will abut each other, a little like partial quantisation.

Alternatively, you can make the notes fully legato and then use a Transform function to reduce their length a little.

❑ Fading with a MIDI Mixer

A common requirement is for a song to fade in or out. The easiest way to do this is to use Controller 7 (Volume) or 11 (Expression). It's even easier if your sequencer has a MIDI Mixer which, fortunately, an increasing number have.

If you can link faders so moving one will also move others in the link, use this to perform the fade. Record the fade on a separate track to make it easier to edit.

If you can't link the faders in your Mixer, just fade out one channel. This may take a little practise as the sounds of the others will be distracting. Copy this track to other tracks and use a Transform function to change the MIDI channels to those of the other parts you want to fade. If your sequencer has a track parameters box you could use this to set the MIDI channel rather than using Transform.

Sometimes, due to the nature of the sounds, a channel may have to be faded more quickly or slowly than the others. Use the Remix or

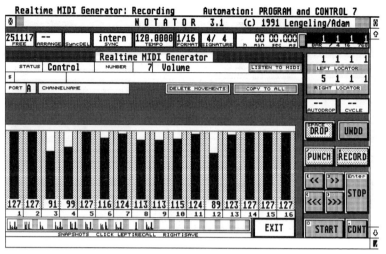

Notator's RMG (Realtime MIDI Generator) can act as a MIDI Mixer and record realtime fader movements into a track.

Demix by Channel function to put each of the fades on a separate track. Mute the offending channel and you can then fade it individually and record it onto another track. I prefer not to delete data until I'm sure I won't need it.

❏ A wheel fade out

If your sequencer has no MIDI Mixer, you may be faced with the prospect of entering a mass of Volume data manually in the event editor. If you sequencer has a mapping function, however, you may be able to map the pitch bend or modulation wheel to Volume and use the wheel to create the fade.

❏ Scaled fades

Some sequencers have a Scale Controller function which will automatically generate an increasing or decreasing range of controller data across a specified number of bars. Some even have linear and exponential curve changes. Try this with Volume or Expression to produce automatic fades.

I've had a degree of success with this but it may well be that the fade doesn't sound quite right to you. We don't feel these things in purely linear or exponential terms so you may have to resort to some manual adjustments.

Notator's Transform function will scale Volume data – or any other
Controller – to produce smooth fades.

☑ PROJECT

Pseudo crossfades

Several synths have facilities such as morphing and vector synthesis in
which the one sound changes into another one over time as you play a
note. The results can be very dramatic. If you don't have such an
instrument you can duplicate the effect to an extent using Volume or
Expression.

Record a part and copy it to another track. Set the tracks to
different MIDI channels and select suitable sounds. The idea is to fade
one track down while fading the other track up using Volume or
Expression data.

Ideally, you should use a Scale Volume function to make sure the
fades are even. You can draw them in by hand using a Graphic
Controller editor but this is a little more difficult. Some sequencers
have a Scale Velocity function which you can use but bear in mind the
differences between Velocity and Volume mentioned earlier in this
section.

Set the scale range to cover the length of the section you want to
affect. Try a Volume range from, say, 127 to 15 on the fade out and, vice
versa on the fade in. If you want to fade the sound completely, then set
the lower limit to 0. If you are using Velocity, you may want to make the
upper value 100. The actual values required will vary with the sounds

used so a little experimentation will probably be required.

If your sequencer has a Reverse function which reverses all events and not just notes, use it to produce an exact mirror image of the fade out. It is also a good idea to record the Controller changes on separate tracks so you can mute them and edit them without disturbing the original data.

This technique can produce pretty dramatic effects with long notes which give the sound time to change. Especially effective are patches which are rich in harmonics although you can use the process with any sound.

However, it also works with any music line. With a lead line, for example, the lead sound will change from one tone to another. In fact, you can create very interesting effects using short fade ins and outs which will make the music line crossfade between sounds very rapidly. This will be much easier to set up and monitor if you use separate tracks for the Controller data.

Create a 'fade patch' which fades the volume down and then up again, say over a bar or two. The complementary patch, of course, will fade the volume up and then down. When you've got the right mix, copy the two patches across the length of the phrases you want to affect.

☑ PROJECT

Multi pseudo crossfades

If you like the results the previous project produces, you can take the process a stage further and crossfade between three, four or more sounds. It takes a little more setting up but the results can be even more spectacular as the music shifts from one tone to another.

There are numerous permutations to try. For example, with a three-sound crossfade, you could simply make the sounds take turns to fade in and out one after the other.

Bar	1	2	3	4	5	6	7	
Track 1	In	Out	Off	In	Out	Off	In	
Track 2	Out	Off	In	Out	Off	In	Out	
Track 3	Off	In	Out	Off	In	Out	Off	

If you dispense with the Off phase and extend the fade across three bars, the sounds will fade in and out, slightly offset against each other.

Bar	1	2	3	4	5	6	7	8
Track 1	In		Out		In		Out	
Track 2	In		Out		In		Out	
Track 3	Out		In		Out		In	

The options increase if you use four sounds. Of course, the fades don't have to be regular. You could offset them so one part fades in and out every two bars, another every three bars and another every four bars. In this instance the fades would repeat themselves every 12 bars. With fades over bars of other lengths you could create fade cycles lasting dozens of bars.

☑ PROJECT

Pan crossfades

Use a similar process to the above but with MIDI Controller 10 (Pan) to create pan sweeps which will swirl the phrase around the stereo image as it plays. (See the entry on *Dynamic panning* in Chapter 12 for more info about the limits of panning sounds.)

If you have created Volume or Expression fades from the previous Project, use your sequencer's Transform function to change the Controller to 10 and you have a ready-made Pan effect.

If you only have a single music line, you only need one pan patch. However, you could combine pan sweeps with crossfades. For example, the two sounds could be in the middle of the stereo position when they are at the same volume and move out towards the edges as they fade or vice versa. You could offset the pan movement in relation to the crossfade so each time the sounds meet they are at different places in the stereo image.

❏ Adding depth

Nothing fills a sound out more than adding a smattering of reverb. It's a shame they don't produce sequencers with built-in reverb but there you are. So if you want a more spacious sound, get an FX unit. Adding reverb to beef-up a sound is an age-old panacea, very effective, but don't overdo it.

Composition

The original purpose of sequencers was simply to record and play back music, but as they acquired more features they became able to add to and assist in the creative process. Cubase, for example, has a very interesting module called the IPS (Interactive Phrase Synthesiser) which can modify music data in all sorts of ways. There also several stand-alone programs which are worth exploring if you're interested in computer-assisted composition. However, these are beyond the scope of this book.

Here we'll look at ways of using standard sequencer functions to aid the composition process.

☑ PROJECT

Note reversal

Your sequencer either has a Reverse Notes feature or it hasn't. Reversing the notes in a musical phrase is an old trick used by many classical composers but it can work surprisingly well with more modern material, too.

Try it with bass lines and drum patterns. You don't have to apply it to an entire track. In fact, you will probably get more usable results if you apply it to two- or four-bar phrases.

It can be particularly effective with long runs of regular notes. Try it with some Bach. You can further process the result by apply a swing quantise or groove to it (see the *Quantisation* section in Chapter 6 for more about this).

☑ PROJECT

Cyclic compositions 1

If your sequencer has a Double/Half Tempo function you can create ambient/cyclic/minimal compositions. To illustrate the process here's a piece called *There & Back* which is not totally unlike the sort of compositions you can produce with programs such as Dr. T's M. The piece is constructed from only five notes:

1) Record a pattern which we'll assume is on Track 1. Start with a one-bar pattern until you become familiar with the process. If you want a reasonably harmonic piece, use notes which form a chord such as those in the example above.

2) Copy the bar to create a pattern 16 bars long.

3) Copy this to Track 2 (don't use ghost tracks) and apply a Half Tempo function to it so the notes have doubled in duration and the pattern is 32 bars long.

4) Copy the original to Track 3. Apply a Double Tempo function so the notes are half their original duration and the pattern becomes 8 bars long.

5) Copy Track 2 to Track 4 and apply a Half Tempo function so the pattern is 64 bars long.

6) Copy Track 3 to Track 5 and apply Double Tempo so the pattern is 4 bars long.

7) Copy Track 4 to Track 6 and apply Half Tempo so the pattern is 128 bars long.

8) Copy Track 5 to Track 7 and apply Half Tempo so the pattern is 2 bars long. If you used the original example, the shortest notes it will contain will be 1/64th notes.

9) Now comes the interesting bit. You can arrange the patterns in any order you like. The *There & Back* arrangement introduces the patterns one at a time and then removes them on a last-in first-out basis hence the name. The music goes There – to its turning point – and comes Back again to the start.

To duplicate this exactly, continue as follows:

10) Copy the pattern in Track 1 to itself six times (you can use ghost tracks for this) to create a total track length of 112 bars.

11) Copy the pattern in Track 2 to itself twice and move it forward so it starts on bar 9.

12) Make 9 copies of the pattern on Track 3 and move the start to bar 17.

13) Move the pattern on Track 4 to start on bar 25.

14) Make 11 copies of the pattern on Track 5 and move it to start at bar 33.

15) Track 6 is too long so cut it back to 32 bars and move it so it starts at bar 41.

16) Make 7 copies of the pattern on Track 7 and move the start to bar 49.

You should now have a pyramid structure like this:

To complete the arrangement, select suitable sounds for each of the tracks, transpose them and pan them. The original piece used the following settings with sounds based on GM:

Track	Instrument	Tran	Pan
1	Celesta	0	0
2	Cello	-36	-20
3	Grand Piano	12	20
4	Square Wave	-24	-40
5	Pizz Strings	24	40
6	Calliope	-12	-64
7	Glockenspiel	12	63

The There & Back ethos is further enhanced by these settings because the second track plays the notes at twice the duration and at a lower octave. The third track plays the notes with a shorter duration and at a higher octave and so on, and each track is panned to alternating left and right positions in the stereo image.

That's the basic principle. Of course, you could use a different pattern on each track and you don't have to double or half the note durations in exactly the same way.

❑ Cyclic compositions 2

A few sequencers such as Procyon Pro not only let you double and half the note durations but also let you change them by a percentage amount. This is almost the same thing as allowing you to play different tracks at different tempos. If your sequencer has this function, create a track of eight bars, say, playing a simple scale. Copy it to another track and apply a percentage change of 99% to it. Play the two tracks together and you will notice them slowly slipping out of time with each other.

You can use this to create pieces containing some interesting rhythmic changes. Used subtly, you could create a piece in which the music lines slowly fade in and out of sync with each other. At other extremes, the world of avant garde music could be in for a complete shake-up!

☑ *PROJECT*

Creating an analogue sequencer

If you are over 30 you probably remember analogue sequencers. They bore very little resemblance to the sequencers of today but the knobs and dials had an enduring fascination. They were used on many albums by synth pioneers such as Tangerine Dream, Kraftwerk and Jean-Michel Jarre.

Now you can turn your high tech digital sequencer into an old analogue device. There's progress for you! You can adapt the principle to any sequencer but it works best and is most flexible with one which uses patterns and which has a Track Parameters box.

To make a basic 8-step sequencer, create a pattern a quarter note long on track 1 and record a quarter note into, say Middle C. Copy this to tracks 2 to 8, offsetting it by a quarter note on each track so you effectively have eight consecutive notes staggered over eight tracks with a total duration of two bars.

Now set the sequencer to loop the two bars and press play. The result will be totally monotonous. However, if you select each pattern in turn you can use the Transpose setting in the Track Parameters box to change the pitch.

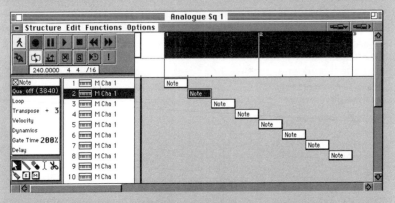

Turning Notator Logic into an analogue sequencer.

As each note is on a different track, you can assign them to different MIDI channels and different sounds. There are various other 'features' you can add, depending on your sequencer's facilities.

Some analogue sequencers had a gate time control which let you alter the on time of the notes. Some modern sequencers such as Notator Logic have a similar control in their Playback Parameters box so you can duplicate this effect. You can even apply different gate times to each note.

Some analogue devices had a length control which let you specify the duration of each note. You can duplicate this effect by selecting the patterns which follow the step whose length you want to increase and dragging them *en masse* further down the timeline, say by a quarter note.

If the loop is still set to two bars, this will put the last note outside the loop. You can adjust the length of the loop if you wish, but that would put the length into odd time signature territory. Which is fine – experimentation is the name of the game, after all. However, if you leave the loop point where it is, that will ensure that any sequences you set up are two bars long – and like it or not, most people prefer music with a regular time signature.

If you try this, you may find that the extended note sounds rather short, particularly if you are using a sound which doesn't have much sustain. That's not surprising as the note is only a quarter note long and there is a quarter note gap after it and before the start of the next note. But we can alter this with the gate time function by setting it to 200%.

I know a guy who had great fun turning his £400 sequencer into an analogue machine but I also know some people who look upon this as a step backwards. Why bother?

It's simply to put a different perspective on the creative process. Using equipment in alternative ways can be enlightening and inspirational. And if you actually used an analogue sequencer all those years ago you may just feel the pangs of nostalgia. Primitive it may be by current standards but that didn't stop TD producing some ground-breaking music.

☑ PROJECT

Open the gate

Gate effects are typically created in the studio using a device called a Noise Gate. This opens and closes according to the level of the signal it receives. When it opens it lets a signal through.

Hooking one up to a drum kit, for example, would make the gate open and close in time with the hits, creating a rhythmic pulse which follows the rhythm pattern. Feed a guitar or synth patch into the Gate and play a chord and the Gate will chop the chord up to match the rhythmic pulse. This can produce very exciting riffs and grooves and is a favourite effect with dance record producers.

You can create similar gate effects with your sequencer using our friend Volume (Controller 7) or Expression (Controller 11). The basic idea is simple – to create a rhythmic arrangement of on/off messages and apply them to a sound.

Here's an example from one of the gate effects on Keyfax Software's *Twiddly Bits* disk, used with kind permission.

Position	Status	Chn	1st	2nd	Description
1:1:1	Control	1	7	127	Volume
1:1:2	Control	1	7	37	Volume
1:1:3	Control	1	7	127	Volume
1:1:4	Control	1	7	127	Volume
1:2:1	Control	1	7	37	Volume
1:2:2	Control	1	7	127	Volume
1:2:3	Control	1	7	37	Volume
1:2:4	Control	1	7	127	Volume
1:3:1	Control	1	7	37	Volume
1:3:2	Control	1	7	127	Volume
1:3:3	Control	1	7	37	Volume
1:3:4	Control	1	7	37	Volume
1:4:1	Control	1	7	127	Volume
1:4:2	Control	1	7	37	Volume
1:4:3	Control	1	7	127	Volume
1:4:4	Control	1	7	37	Volume

The position is the position of the controller messages in bars:beats:sub-beat format. The sub-beats in this case are 1/4 notes. The example above is the first bar of an eight-bar pattern in which the rhythmic pulse in the following bars evolves along similar lines. Enter this data into your sequencer in the Event editor and for convenience copy it to create four bars.

Record a chord on MIDI channel 1 on a separate track and set it to play with a sound rich in harmonics. A sweep pad is ideal. When you play it, you will hear the sort of effects this process can produce. Here's another example from *Twiddly Bits 2*:

Position	Status	Chn	1st	2nd	Description
1:1:1	Control	1	7	127	Volume
1:1:1	Control	1	10	0	Pan
1:1:2	Control	1	7	0	Volume
1:1:3	Control	1	7	127	Volume
1:1:4	Control	1	7	0	Volume
1:2:1	Control	1	7	57	Volume

1:2:2	Control	1	7	0	Volume
1:2:3	Control	1	7	127	Volume
1:2:4	Control	1	7	0	Volume
1:3:1	Control	1	7	127	Volume
1:3:1	Control	1	10	32	Pan
1:3:2	Control	1	7	0	Volume
1:3:3	Control	1	7	57	Volume
1:3:4	Control	1	7	0	Volume
1:4:1	Control	1	7	127	Volume
1:4:2	Control	1	7	0	Volume
1:4:3	Control	1	7	127	Volume
1:4:4	Control	1	7	0	Volume
2:1:1	Control	1	7	57	Volume
2:1:1	Control	1	10	64	Pan

This time Pan has been mixed with Volume. The original is eight-bars long and the sound pans from one side to the other and back again as the sequence plays. To save trees we've only listed the first bar here. Copy it four or eight times but adjust the Pan setting so the sound travels across the stereo image. However, read the next entry for more info about Pan messages before you begin to think that something isn't working!

Creating a gate effect in Notator Logic's Event List.

You can mix modulation data with the gate effect and even combine, pan and modulation. Even more interesting things happen when you create several gate effects and run them simultaneously to produce complex crossrhythms.

You can also use the gates with two or more different sounds. Pan one from left to right and the other from right to left. The possibilities are enormous.

If your sequencer has an Event editor, you can create your own gate effects quite easily although if you want some ready-to-go, get a copy of *Twiddly Bits 2*.

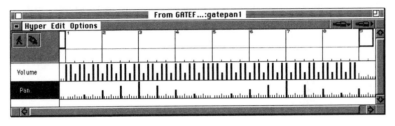

You can see the relationship between the volume and pan instructions in Notator Logic's Hyper Editor.

❑ Dynamic panning problems

If you try the previous Project and record a single chord lasting for the duration of the effect, you may find that the panning does not work. That's because the MIDI spec does not allow you to change the pan position of a sound once it has been triggered. Strange but true.

You can alter the volume of an active sound but dynamic panning is not provided for in the MIDI spec. Shame, because it can be used to create some great effects.

Alternatively, you may find that it does work! Some instruments, including some GS-compatible ones, do support dynamic panning. You'll know if yours does. If it doesn't, then try runs of 1/16th notes - you can really make these whiz around the speakers.

❑ Making major minor

Some songs create a distinctive mood by switching from a major to a minor key or vice versa. You can change a melody or chord progression from major to minor by flattening certain notes. For example, to change C major into C minor involves flattening the B, E and A.

We could get a little more technical by discussing harmonic and melodic minor modes. In particular, if a melody line contains a B natural which leads to a C note, it may be better to leave this alone. However, you can make changes to a certain group of notes and if an individual note doesn't sound quite right you can edit it manually. The following procedure offers a quick way to see how the change would affect a piece of music.

If your sequencer allows you to select specific events for processing, select the B, E and A notes and transpose them down by a semitone.

If it can't do this but it has a Strip Data function, remove these notes and put them on another track. Exactly how you do this will depend on your sequencer. For example, you may be able to extract them, perhaps one note at a time, and paste them into another track. You may be even be able to 'demix' them directly from one track to another. When the notes have been removed, merge them into a single track and transpose it down a semitone.

To convert minor to major, you simply reverse the process and transpose the notes up a semitone.

If you keep the thirds on their own track, you can switch between major and minor modes to compare the differences.

☑ PROJECT

Creative quantisation

Here's a slightly off-the-wall idea which is a few degrees better than random note generation. Take a very busy part, preferably one recorded in realtime. Quantise it to 1/16th or 1/8th notes or to triplets. You can even try 1/4 notes.

I've achieved good results by heavily quantising music lines produced by Fractal Music Composer, an algorithmic composition program. It's a very interesting program to work with because you can define the harmonic structure of the music lines it produces. However, some of the rhythms can be a little irregular which is where positive quantisation comes in.

Even in the absence of a note-generation program, try heavily quantising some of your busier music parts. This will probably result in some horrendous chords as adjacent notes are forced onto the same beat.

Use a Strip function or a High or Low Note Limit function to remove extra notes. It's not guaranteed to produce a masterpiece but it might just produce some interesting ideas you can work with.

☑ *PROJECT*

Drum transposing

You will usually want to preserve your drum parts by protecting the drum track or drum channel against transposition (see the *Transposition* section, Chapter 8, for more info). However, interesting effects can be achieved by deliberately transposing the drum track. The rhythm will usually remain the same (unless you transpose it out of the range of recognised drums) but the drum sounds will change.

Using a GM kit as an example, if you transpose a drum track up a semitone, Bass Drum 1 will become Bass Drum 2, Snare 1 will become a Hand Clap, closed Hi Hat will become a Low Tom and the Ride Cymbal will become a Tambourine. The change in emphasis can be quite enlightening.

If you have each drum on its own track you can be even more creative. For example, you might like to keep the bass and snare the same but try different drum sounds for the hi hat or tom tom line.

This technique can produce particularly interesting results when you move the drum track higher than Middle C (MIDI note 60) where most of the ethnic sounds reside.

☑ *PROJECT*

Off-the-wall drum patterns

Ever accidentally assigned a music line to the drum channel? Was it good? Bass lines, for example, can sound very interesting when played with drum sounds.

Assign some of your non-drum parts to the drum channel and see what comes out. In fact, assign two non-drum parts to the drum channel. Quantise them to 1/16th or 1/32nd notes or try quantising them to different values, even triplets. Some fascinating rhythms and drum combinations can emerge here, although if you have lots of high notes be prepared for hefty use of the Samba Whistle!

The object is to inspire rather than to discover a whole new ready-to-use pattern so be prepared to get in there and edit.

13 Keyboard tips

Although MIDI is oriented towards keyboards, they can create certain problems of their own.

❏ Velocity as volume

Some older synthesisers simply don't respond to Volume data so in spite of everything we've said about Volume, Expression and Velocity, the only way to tweak the volume is to use Velocity. Most sequencers let you apply a Velocity offset to a track so that's generally not a major problem.

❏ Splitting right and left hand parts

Many keyboard players find it easier to play the left and right hands together than to play them separately. Sometimes, however, you may want to split a keyboard performance into left and right hands to assign them to different sounds. There are a number of ways to do this.

1) Some sequencers with a score editor let you draw in a division between the left and right hands. This is particularly useful when the left hand plays high notes which stray into the right hand's half of the keyboard.
2) Many keyboards have a zoning facility which lets you select a split point and assign the high and low sections to different MIDI channels. Record this and them demix the MIDI channels onto two separate tracks.
3) Use a grid editor and find the highest note played by the left hand. Select this and all the notes below it. Cut it and paste it into another track.

These last two methods assume that the two hands don't overlap into each other's territory. If they do you have a little more editing to do. Let's retrieve the left-hand notes first. Copy the sections which contain overlapping notes to a spare track. Go into an editor of your choice, delete the notes played by the right hand and paste the rest into the left hand track. Use a similar process to extract the right-hand parts.

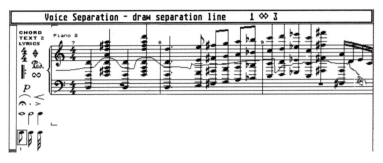

Notator lets you split left and right hand parts by drawing a line between them.

❏ More realistic guitar bends

Twiddling the pitch bend wheel during a screaming guitar solo is fun and it can be very expressive but it does not always produce the most realistic results. There are a couple of things you can do to improve the realism.

1) Guitars can only bend the pitch upwards so make sure that the wheel doesn't bend the pitch downwards.

2) Guitarists often bend the pitch upwards a semitone so set a semitone pitch bend limit on your guitar patch.

Guitar tips

It's almost impossible to record authentic guitar parts on a keyboard and there are times when nothing less than a MIDI guitar will do. However, this data needs to be handled in a different way to a keyboard recording.

❑ Quantising MIDI guitar parts

Because guitars are strummed, they can generate a series of notes whose start times vary only slightly, often less than 1/64th note. If you quantise this you remove an element of what makes it a guitar recording. So first of all, remove any record quantise setting.

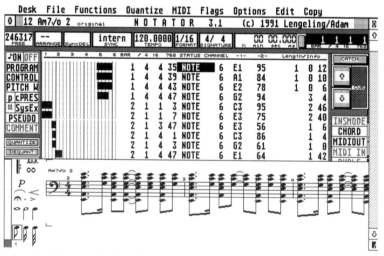

These look like straight chords but you can see from the event list that the notes are offset – they have been strummed. Quantising this would ruin the feel.

If the timing is out and you feel you must quantise, try doing it by hand. Select the piano roll editor and switch off any 'snap to' function.

Select the notes in the chord and drag them to the required position. Zoom in to do this as accurately as possible. This will help correct the timing while preserving the strum effect.

If the note lengths are wrong, you can safely quantise them.

❑ Removing unwanted pitch bend

MIDI guitars often generate unwanted pitch bend data as the slightest movement of a string triggers the pitch-to-MIDI converter. It does not generally cause a problem but it does use memory and contribute to the MIDI data flow.

If you want rid of it, look at the pitch bend data in a graphic editor. The spurious data will usually consist of very low values and will flutter about on either side of the zero line without forming an obvious pitch bend shape. Highlight it and delete it.

❑ Multichannel recording

One of the useful aspects of a MIDI guitar is that in mono mode it can transmit each string on a different MIDI channel which can make editing a lot easier and it gives you scope for more creative editing.

Some sequencers have a multichannel record mode which automatically puts each channel on a different track. If your sequencer doesn't, record everything onto one track and use the Split by Channel or Demix function to put each string on its own track.

Cubase's Multirecord function has several options.

Sequencing live

The ultimate aim of many musicians as they construct and arrange songs on their sequencer is to take them on the road and use them for live gigs. Here are a few tips which may make the process a little easier.

❏ Gigging with a sequencer

The first tip simply has to be – don't take your sequencer on the road! Well, it's not so much the sequencer as the computer and associated equipment it runs on. Computers, monitors and hard disks weren't designed to be lugged around. Even a well-padded flight case will afford little protection if it falls off the stage or off a table. But if you must, make sure you have cases specially designed for the job. Some companies produce rack-mount units for computers which is a good idea.

❏ Using a hardware sequencer or MIDI file player

A more reliable way to use MIDI files live is to create the arrangements on your computer, save them as Standard MIDI Files and play them on a hardware sequencer or MIDI file player. These are designed for life on the road and are much more sturdy.

Apart from that, MIDI file players play files directly from disk so there is no waiting time as a song loads, unlike a traditional sequencer.

If you have an ST, another option is to use *OnStage* from Hands On. The pack includes a piece of software and a box containing LEDs which lets you use the ST for playing MIDI files without a monitor.

❏ Backup safety net

Whichever system of MIDI file playback you use, take a spare set of disks with you. You'll almost certainly need them one day.

❏ Be prepared for failure

Expect the best but be prepared for the worst, as the saying goes. One day, even if you treat your computer equipment with kidd gloves, you may plug it in, turn it on and get a blank screen. Carry a MIDI file player or a DAT or cassette player with audio recordings of your backing tracks as backup.

❏ Creating a flexible set

Occasionally it will be necessary to alter the length or content of your set. You may want to respond spontaneously to the audience or you may get the wind-up sign from the management – if the act before you overran! To make your set as flexible as possible, keep each song on a separate disk or prepare alternative combinations of songs. Make your routine flexible.

❏ A third hand

Having warned you of some of the potential problems of using MIDI files live, there are also many advantages. As well as providing a backing band, they can also be used to change sounds in your equipment, exactly on cue. They can control audio mixers as well as MIDI mixers and they can send Sys Ex dumps to load a new set of sounds into a synth. This leaves you completely free to concentrate on the performance.

❏ MIDI lighting

Lighting is now an essential part of virtually all live gigs, even those in small venues. There are several affordable MIDI lighting systems on the market. The advantage is that you can insert commands to control the lighting in the song files so they themselves do all the hard work. You can be very creative and produce effects in perfect synchronisation with the songs.

❏ Vocal spacemen

If you use MIDI files to control an effects unit which you also use for vocals, at the end of every file insert a command to zero the effects setting. This ensures that when you thank the audience for their tumultuous round of applause that you don't do so in a voice swamped with echo. Presumably, you will also insert effects settings at the beginning of each file. If so, the MIDI files can totally control the effects settings so you don't have to worry about stomping on the effect unit's on/off button between songs. However, it may be a good idea to have a manual override switch somewhere just in case a sequence is interrupted.

❏ Improvising with MIDI files

One of the drawbacks with MIDI files is that you can't shout at them: 'Once more round the chorus, chaps'. Well, you can but it won't take any notice! However, there are ways of accomplishing similar results with a computer. Macros!

These are a series of commands which you can trigger by pressing a single combination of keys. For example, you could create a macro to mute the instrumental tracks and activate the loop command to cycle around the last chorus. If the song is going well, you can do drum and vocal repeats of the chorus and get the audience to join in.

You could create a macro to load and start playing a file or even select one of a number of alternative arrangements by selectively muting various tracks.

You can record macros on a PC using Windows' Recorder accessory.

There is a macro routine built into Windows on the PC and there are stand-alone macro programs for the Mac such as QuickKeys or the shareware KeyQuencer.

❑ Voice control

This may seem a little futuristic but it's possible to put your sequencer - or any other program for that matter - under voice control. The technology is now quite sophisticated and there are programs such as Voice Navigator for the Mac which can filter out ambient noise.

All voice commands do, in effect, is trigger macros, but think about the possibilities for a moment before you dismiss this. Imagine loading and playing a song, looping a chorus, muting a track or changing sound purely by giving a vocal command.

For a more interactive set, a single word in conversation with the audience, for example, could trigger a reaction - music, light or any other MIDI-controllable effect.

❑ Recording good ideas

Most musicians probably think of a sequencer as a means of playing data on a gig but you can also use one to record your performance. Have you ever played a solo live which, due to the buzz, was simply the best thing you've ever done? It's lost. Hook your instrument up to a sequencer and set it to record instead of playback and you can capture your live inspirations.

Files

As with all computer applications, you must save your work to disk to avoid it being relegated to the great RAM wilderness when you switch off your machine. Files also give you the means of transferring music from one computer to another and enable it to be played on MIDI file players.

❑ Save often
It just needs someone to trip over a plug or a power cut or spike to occur and you could lose hours of work. And even the most stable computer system can throw a wobbler and crash. Protect your music by saving often. I'm paranoid about losing work and save it after every major change. It doesn't take half a second. If your sequencer has a hot key combination for Save, learn it and use it.

❑ Save everything
Squirrels will probably do this anyway. During the initial stages of your composition you will probably create several alternate music lines. If something has merit, even if it doesn't fit your present composition, save it. When the work is finished you can go back, listen to the out-takes and keep any which you like. They may just find a home in another project.

❑ Back it up
Backup your work. If you are working with a hard disk, backup your work to a floppy. If you're using floppies, make a copy. It's a chore but you only have to lose data once by not backing it up and you'll backup from that point onward. Forever.

❑ All-in-one storage
Most instruments with programmable voices can execute a bulk dump which will transmit all their sound data via MIDI. This is usually used by a voice editor or librarian although many musicians store their sequence data on one disk and voice data on another.

However, if your sequencer can record Sys Ex data, consider storing both music and voice data in the same file, at least when the song is complete. This has the advantage of keeping all the song data in one place so you don't have to hunt through your box of synth patches to find the sounds you used for a song.

If you need to edit the song at a later date, once it has been loaded and the instruments setup, remove the Sys Ex data because you don't want to transmit it each time you play the song. This is easiest done if your sequencer is pattern based. You can either mute the pattern or save it to disk, ready to load and merge into the song again when you've finished the session.

While some sequencers treat Sys Ex data just as if it was any other type of MIDI data, others have a special Sys Ex record mode which saves the data direct to disk.

Others simply ignore Sys Ex data altogether in which case it may be worth investing in a librarian for your synth. If your sequencer can't handle Sys Ex data but you have a librarian, store the sequence data and voice data in the same folder on the same disk.

❏ Standard MIDI files

If you are saving files to disk for use with a MIDI file player, save them in Format 0. Most sequencers can read both Format 0 (all MIDI channels on one track) and Format 1 (MIDI channels on separate tracks) files but many MIDI file players can read only Format 0 files, which is slightly more efficient when files are being played directly from disk. Most current machines, however, can also read Format 1 files.

```
┌─────────────────────────────────────────┐
│           MIDI File Options              │
│  ─────────────────────────────────────   │
│  Export                                   │
│    MIDI file type                         │
│        ○ Type 1 - Multiple tracks         │
│        ● Type 0 - Single multi-channel track │
│        ○ Type 0 - Conductor track only    │
│    ☐ Export markers as lyrics             │
│  Import                                    │
│      ☐ Import lyrics as markers           │
│      ☒ Put initial volume and program change │
│        into track sheet (Type 1 files only) │
│                                           │
│   ( Cancel )              [  OK  ]        │
└─────────────────────────────────────────┘
```

Mastertracks Pro lets you choose from several MIDI file options.

Also, most file players cannot read the contents of a directory so make sure all files are in the root portion of the disk.

❏ **Transferring files between computers**

If you want to give your Meisterwerk to someone else who has a different computer system, you need two things - (1) a mutually-compatible file format and (2) a mutually-compatible transfer medium. (1) Standard MIDI files usually do the job quite well. Few modern sequencers will throw a wobbler over any kind of MIDI data although some older ones may wince at Sys Ex, tempo events or certain kinds of controller data. Many sequencers are now available on several computer platforms and can read data generated by their stable mates. (2) The usual transfer medium is a floppy disk. Most computers can, with a little help, read MS DOS disks as used by PCs. PCs obviously can, but make sure you don't use a high density disk unless you're sure the receiving machine can read it.

Most Atari STs can read and write PC disks although there is a certain grey area here which centres around the ST's and the PC's operating systems. Although an ST should be able to read a PC disk, it cannot create (format) one but there are several ST utilities in the Public Domain which enable it to format an MS DOS disk.

Public Domain programs are software which can be freely copied and distributed. They are available from PD libraries which charge a nominal copying fee. PD libraries advertise widely in computer magazines.

The Commodore Amiga needs a utility to enable it to read MS DOS disks. The cheapest and the best is probably Messy SID, another PD program.

The Acorn Archimedes can read MS DOS disks directly although older models need a utility such as MultiFS to do so.

The new Apple Macs come with a piece of software which lets them read and write PC disks although older machines will need a utility such as DOS Mounter or Access PC. The Mac also needs to be equipped with a SuperDrive which has been fitted to all Macs since 1989.

There's another slight complication with Macs and that is Mac files have a File Type and a Creator Type. These are attributes attached to the file which enable you to launch an application which created a document by double clicking on the document. When you give a MIDI file to a Mac it is devoid of this information. Some sequencers will try to load it anyway, but with many it won't even show up in the file dialogue box.

The solution is simple. You need to give it a file type. The creator type is not so important but you may as well match that to your sequencer anyway.

You can do this via the MS DOS reader utility which will assign a file and creator type to an incoming file based on its extension. This is

Access PC lets you assign a creator and file type to a DOS extension. Here, PC MIDI files will automatically be recognised as Cubase files.

three characters tagged onto the end of a filename and the PC equivalent of the Mac's file type. MIDI files have the extension MID. There are also PD programs such as File Typer and MIDI File Converter which will stamp the necessary attributes onto the files.

❑ Transferring files the hard way

If you have a couple of computers which refuse to read each other's disks or if you want to transfer a file from a workstation or hardware sequencer with its own disk format, you can transfer files by linking them via MIDI and playing a file from one while recording it on the other.

The obvious way to do this is to make the playing sequencer the master and set it to transmit MIDI clock, and make the recording sequencer the slave set up with external synchronisation. However, you may get better accuracy if you reverse the roles. To do this you have to connect both MIDI leads, that is, the MIDI In and Out from one computer must be connected to the MIDI Out and In respectively of the other.

After transferring a file in this way, examine the data in the event editor. You may find that the events occur a clock tick or two later than they do in the original sequence. This reflects the time taken for the MIDI data to fly down the cable and be recorded. You may be able to correct this using quantise but you only want to do this if the original piece was quantised, too.

You can minimise the clock offset by reducing the tempo during recording. At a very slow tempo you may well get the majority of the data on the beat.

❏ File transfers via comms software

Yet another option is to transfer the files using communications software. The advantage here is that you can send a file instantly to another computer virtually anywhere in the world. If the two computers are next to each other you will need to use a null modem link to join the two. You should then be able to use comms software to link the computers and transfer files.

A full discussion of comms is beyond the scope of this book but if you already use comms this option is worth considering.

Troubleshooting

Although MIDI is a so-called standard it is not implemented in the same way and the same degree on all devices and this can lead to a variety of problems. Hopefully, you won't encounter any serious problems but if you do, this section may help sort them out.

❑ The truth about MIDI delays

Much has been said and written about delays caused by daisy chaining, MIDI Thru sockets and the transmission of excess amounts of MIDI data. Let's look at a few facts.

MIDI is a serial communications protocol which can transmit 31,250 bits of information per second. The following sentence is for the technically-minded - if you don't understand it skip to the next one. MIDI bytes are 8 bits long and each includes 2 extra bits for error checking so there are 10 bits in a MIDI byte. This means that MIDI can send 3 bytes of data every millisecond (1/1000 of a second). Note On messages are three bytes long so it takes about 1 millisecond to send a Note On message and 1 millisecond to send a Note Off message. Therefore - bottom line coming up - MIDI can play around 500 notes per second.

Most people will not experience any noticeable delay until notes are more than 20 milliseconds apart so you can safely play around 16 notes simultaneously although the type of sound used can effect our perception, too.

However, when controller data is used, this can force the notes further apart than 20 milliseconds so a delay does become noticeable. Another contributing factor is the speed at which the receiving instrument can process the data. Synthesisers contain microprocessors just like computers and some are faster than others.

❑ Easing MIDI delay problems

Most delay problems are caused by asking a unit to process more MIDI data than it can handle or by trying to transmit more data than MIDI itself is capable of transmitting. The solution is to cut out or thin down unnecessary data, particularly controller data.

MIDI itself tries to ease the situation with a system called Running

Status although this is not supported by all instruments. Without getting too technical, MIDI messages include a status byte which tells the system what kind of message is about to follow.

Every Note On message, for example, is preceded by a Note On status byte. Running Status allows the system to omit subsequent status bytes so it assumes all further messages are Note On messages until it receives a different status byte. This can considerably reduce the amount of data particularly where large amounts of controller data are being transmitted.

❏ Running Status playback problems

Running Status can cause problems with some older instruments. The Korg DDD1 and DDD5, Sequential Prophet T8, Ensoniq Mirage and some early Yamaha DX7s don't like it and will play back data which uses it very erratically. If you have such an instrument, switch off Running Status in your sequencer's MIDI Filter box.

❏ No sound?

If something isn't playing or recording as it should, there could be several reasons. Some sequencers show MIDI activity (data arriving or data being transmitted) on their tracks and this will at least let you know if the sequencer is generating or receiving data.

Here's a list of other things to check. Some may seem trivial but it's often the obvious which gets overlooked.

1) Ensure the synth or sound module is connected to an amp and speakers and both the amp and the units' volume controls are turned up.

2) Is the MIDI cable okay? The weakest links in a MIDI system are often the cables, especially if they are regularly plugged and unplugged. Test the system with cables which you know work.

3) If MIDI Thru on the sequencer seems not to be working, connect the keyboard directly to the sound module to confirm that both are working correctly.

4) Has the sequencer transmitted a low Volume message to the instrument. If so, it will still transmit MIDI data but the instrument won't produce any sound. The quick way to correct this is to reset the instrument but if your sequencer has a Mixer or a Volume parameter, set it to 127.

5) Check record and transmit Filters as these can mask out certain types of MIDI data.

6) If no sound is coming from a keyboard, check that Local Control

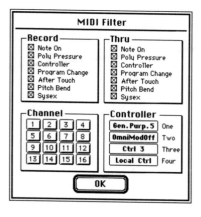

If you don't hear any sound, check your MIDI Filter setting. Something like this wouldn't let anything in or out!

is turned on. (See the MIDI *Thru* entry in Chapter 2 for more info about Local Control.)

7) Is the sound module in a daisy chain? If so, make sure the intervening instruments are switched on otherwise the MIDI datawill not pass through. (See the *Do you need a Thru box or* MIDI *Switcher?* entry in Chapter 2 for more about daisy chains.)

8) Check that the instrument is set to receive on the MIDI channel the data is being transmitted on. If in doubt, set the instrument to Omni mode.

❑ Stuck notes

Stuck notes, sometimes called the Dreaded MIDI Drone, are a perennial hazard with MIDI. They occur when an instrument receives a Note On message without a corresponding Note Off. The first thing to do is stop it.

Many sequencers have a Panic Button which sends an All Notes Off command. Some instruments don't recognise this, however, so some sequencers retaliated by letting you set up the Panic Button to transmit Note Offs for every note on every MIDI channel. It may take longer but it's thorough.

As an alternative to switching the instrument off and on again, press as many notes on the keyboard as you can. This works in two ways. If you hit the right key it will switch the note on and when you release the key it will switch it off. Failing this, if you press enough keys you may use up all the voices (unless you have one of these 64-note polyphonic jobbies) causing the instrument to steal the stuck note, thereby switching it off.

Stuck notes can occur for a number of reasons.

(1) MIDI clog. This can occur if the device receives more data than it can process. If it's helpful enough to flash a MIDI buffer overflow message on its LCD you know this is the problem. Check your sequence and remove or thin out controller data. See the next entry for more about this.

(2) MIDI can only transmit a finite amount of data at one time and if you try to squeeze more data down the cable than it can handle you may lose some. If it's a Note Off message you know what could happen. Again, the solution is to ease the data flow. Remove unnecessary controllers, use a MIDI Thru box instead of a daisy chain system and/or invest in a second MIDI interface which will split the MIDI data flow between two or more MIDI Outs. See the 32 MIDI *channel* entry in Chapter 2 for more info.

(3) A glitch note. This can be a note which is so short that the instrument misses the Note Off part of its message, although most modern instruments don't have this problem. The glitch can occur during editing or transform commands or it can be recorded if you brush a key accidentally during recording. Most modern sequencers are very good at spotting Note Ons which have no corresponding Note Off instructions so such an occurrence should be rare. Glitches can also occur with MIDI guitars.

(4) If you change MIDI channel during playback, the instrument will receive a Note On on one channel and a Note off on another - which won't switch the note off.

❏ Unmute doesn't work

Some sequencers have a Mute command which will switch off its tracks and this can be useful for bringing in a part after a few bars, for example. If you are using this feature and the track does not respond to the Unmute command, check where you have placed these instructions!

Many sequencer users put control data such as volume in the track it is to affect. If you have put the Mute and Unmute commands there, Unmute will not work. Why? Because the track is muted!

If you use Mute, dedicate a separate track to it. If your sequencer doesn't have many tracks, then combine it with other controller data such as Volume.

❏ Mute and delay problems with standard MIDI files

Standard MIDI files were developed to allow sequences to be transferred between different sequencers. However, not all sequencers convert the files in the same way. For example, if a sequence contains muted tracks or tracks which have been delayed using a Track Parameters setting, will the SMF include muted and delayed tracks?

Good question. The answer depends on the sequencer. Some will convert a delayed track into real MIDI data by offsetting the data it contains. Others may not. Likewise, a track which has been muted may or may not appear in the SMF. Cubase, for example, does not save muted tracks which is a sensible approach.

If you suspect that an SMF is not the way it should be, check the original file if possible. Similarly, if you are creating an SMF for use by others, apply all real-time parameters to the tracks so you physically alter the data. Many sequencers have a Normalise function which does this.

❑ Wrong bend

Does the pitch bend in a sequence sound wrong? Perhaps it's supposed to go up a semitone and it goes up a tone. Chances are the pitch bend range in the receiving instrument is not the same as the one used to record it.

The easiest solution is to set the pitch bend response in both recording and receiving instruments to the same amount.

If you have two instruments whose pitch bend ranges seem incompatible or if you have a pre-recorded sequence where the pitch bend is out of whack with your equipment, use a Scale function to tone down the pitch bend data. As a last resort you may have to edit the pitch bend data manually. This will be easiest in a graphic controller editor.

❑ Weird sounds at the extremities of the pitch range

Some instruments do not support MIDI's full 128-note range and if you instruct them to play notes outside their range, the result may not be what you expect. Check an instrument's note range by looking at the MIDI Implementation Chart which is usually in the back of the instruction manual.

The way instruments respond to notes outside their range varies. A common response is to 'fold back' the notes so they play at the highest possible octave although some instruments may simply ignore notes outside their range.

❑ Double voices

When you play your keyboard it plays double notes or the sounds seem thin or as if they've been through a flanger. This is caused by the notes played being echoed through the sequencer's MIDI Thru system so the keyboard is actually playing two sets of notes. The solution is to switch Local Control Off. For more info about this see the MIDI *Thru* entry in Chapter 2.

❑ **Not enough polyphony**

You have a 24-voice polyphonic sound module but it won't play more than 16 or 20 music lines.

The problem here lies in the definition of the term 'voice'. To most musicians a voice is a single sound-producing element rather like a single singer in a choir. However, musical instrument manufacturers use the term to describe a single sound generator, and the patches in many instruments use two or sometimes more voices.

General MIDI instruments are particularly at fault here. If you use sounds which all require two voices, a 24-voice polyphonic instrument would only be able to play 12 notes! In practice, with an average selection of sounds, you will usually have enough polyphony to play 18 or more notes. Instruments which use more than one voice or element in a sound usually list them in the manual so you can check to see exactly how many voices a particular setup is using.

❑ **Notes are cut off**

If notes seem to be disappearing at odd moments, check that you are not exceeding your instrument's polyphony. Even if you are not, check if a certain number of voices, elements or partials have been reserved for any of the music parts. This can reduce the polyphony of other parts.

Check if there are any All Notes Off messages in the sequence. Some instruments actually transmit this message when you release all the keys. If yours is one, use the Input filters to remove it.

❑ **Merging waver**

You've merged a couple of tracks and the sound has become wavery. This can happen when you mix controller data such as modulation or pitch bend from different tracks. Check the controller content of the tracks before merging. Make a backup copy of your music or make sure you can undo the process before you merge.

❑ **Memory problems**

If you are working with a 1Mb ST or Amiga, you may run into memory problems. There are several types of data which can clog up the system which you can remove with no detrimental effect. Aftertouch is one. Check if it is used for any of the sounds and remove it if it isn't. MIDI guitars can generate excess pitch bend data.

Controller data such as pitch bend and modulation which has been recorded in real-time can be quite memory-hungry. Use a Strip or Thin Data function to reduce this. You can remove a significant amount of controller data without it making any noticeable difference to the music.

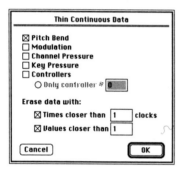

Mastertracks Pro lets you thin any kind of controller data which can help ease memory problems and reduce MIDI clog.

❑ Out of tune synths

Has a music part suddenly gone out of tune? The chances are there is some spurious pitch bend data lying around. Seek and destroy. Make sure controller data at the start of all tracks is set to zero. Either enter neutral controller values at the start of the piece or use reset controller messages. See the *Setting up GM and GS files using Controllers* section in Chapter 3.

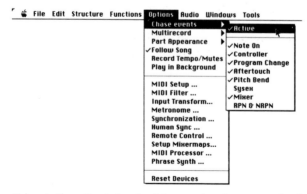

Cubase's Chase Events function lets you select the events to be chased.

If you stopped playback in the middle of a sequence containing pitch bend data it may begin playback at a different pitch. Switch the Chase Controllers function on. This will scan backwards through the sequence so it restarts with the correct controller settings.

❏ Volume dropouts

Does a part suddenly vanish during playback? The chances are the MIDI channel has received a low Volume message. If you use Volume to create a special effect or to balance music parts, make sure to reset it. Be especially careful if you use it to produce a fade out.

❏ Instrument won't change banks

Assuming you are transmitting the correct Bank Select messages (see the tips in Chapter 2), check if the instrument has a Bank Receive Parameter and if so, that it's set to On.

❏ Incorrect sounds

If you are sending a program change number but the sound you expect to play on your instrument is wrong, check that the sequencer and instrument use the same numbering system. See *Dialling the right program number* entry in Chapter 3.

If you have set a program change value in a Track Parameters box, check that there is no program change instruction in the track itself.

❏ Drum machine/external sequencer won't sync

In order to sync two such devices they must support MIDI Clock messages. Check the System Real Time section of the MIDI Implementation Chart. The controlling sequencer must be set to transmit MIDI Clock. Simply setting it to Internal Sync does not always automatically enable MIDI Clock transmission. The receiving device must be set to receive them. Usually, setting it to External Sync will do the job but if that doesn't work, check the manual.

18 *Sequencer Secrets MIDI files disk*

The aim of this book is to help you make better use of your sequencer. To help in this we have assembled a disk of MIDI files containing examples of some of the techniques described in the book. It contains over 30 files including examples from many of the ☑ *PROJECTS* such as Sys Ex messages, MIDI echo, pseudo crossfades, the use of grooves, better hi hat patterns, examples of cyclic compositions, gate effects and the dynamic panning of Flight of the Bumble Bee!

Sequencer Secrets
MIDI files disk

PC Publishing

The disk also includes files from several leading MIDI file production companies. They are full of useful drum patterns, riffs, grooves, rhythms and other data which you can incorporate in your own songs. You can examine the files to see how the professionals approach sequencer programming.

Hands On: Several Rave and Rock drum patterns plus a complete Jazz Funk track.

Heavenly Music: Funky drum patterns, Hit Shot grooves and Brass, Guitar and Sax riffs.

Keyfax Software: Extracts from *Twiddly Bits* and *Twiddly Beats* plus individual, er, twiddly bits.

Newtronic: Fully-arranged demos of Club, Electric, Funky, Reggae and Techno grooves.

Station Records: Full arrangements of authentic acoustic and electric guitar patterns – funky, blues, jazz and Latin guitar – plus drum patterns and Chopin's Minute Waltz.

Words & Music: A collection of drum patterns plus selections from their catalogue of classical music.

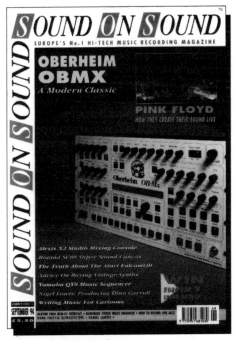

Please note that the Sequencer Secrets disk is available in MS DOS format only. This can be read by virtually all computers although some need a software utility to do so. See the *Transferring files between computers* entry in Chapter 16 for more information. For UK residents the disk is £6.99 (including VAT and p&p). Orders for overseas are £9.49 (Sterling cheque drawn on a UK bank).

Please send cheque, payable to PC Publishing, with order to:

PC Publishing
Export House
130 Vale Road
Tonbridge
Kent TN9 1SP
UK

19 Contacts

MIDI file suppliers

There are probably over two dozen companies selling or producing MIDI files, mostly of rock and pop songs, but we're only listing here the companies which produce building block disks. These contain drum patterns, guitar riffs, grooves and licks which you can use in your own music.

You may be an excellent keyboard player, songwriter or arranger but not so confident about creating drum patterns. And creating convincing guitar licks from a keyboard is not a job for the faint-hearted. So don't be afraid to call in a little help when required.

Hands On MIDI Software, 11 Warfield Avenue, Waterlooville, Hampshire, PO7 7JN. Tel: 01705 783100. Produces a wide range of grooves and drum patterns, and a disk of Sys Ex initialisation and setup messages for GS instruments.

Heavenly Music, 39 Garden Road, Jaywick, Clacton, Essex, CO15 2RT. Tel: 01255 434217. Has an extremely wide and varied collection of drum patterns, dance grooves and jam tracks, also Cubase Mixer Maps.

Keyfax Software, PO Box 4408, Henley-on-Thames, Oxon, RG9 1FS. Tel: 01734 471382. Home of the Twiddly Bits disks - licks and riff for guitar, drums, percussion, string, brass, bass, synth, piano, organ and woodwind sounds recorded by a team of professional players.

Newtronic, 62b Manor Avenue, London, SE4 1TE. Tel: 0181 691 1087. Has a large number of drum pattern disks in styles ranging from Techno to Urban Street Samba.

Station Records, Station Road, Sudbury, Suffolk, CO10 6SS. Tel: 01787 311500. Specialises in electric and acoustic guitar patterns recorded with a MIDI guitar for realism, also some drum patterns recorded using MIDI drum kit.

Words & Music, 15 Falcon Hill, Kirk Hill, Morpeth, Northumberland NE61 2YG. Tel 01670 519589. Specialises in classical music MIDI files but also has a collection of drum patterns.

Music software suppliers

The following companies are the major music software distributors in the UK and the list includes the main software lines they handle. If they don't sell directly to the public they will put you in touch with your nearest supplier. In any event, it's always a good idea to see the software in action before you buy it.

Arbiter Pro MIDI, Wilberforce Road, London, NW9 6AX. Tel: 0181 202 1199. PG Music, Passport, Big Noise, Musicator, Voyetra, Sound Quest.

Clares Micro Supplies, 98 Middlewich Road, Rudheath, Northwich, Cheshire, CW9 7DA. Tel: 01606 48511 Clares Music software for the Acorn Archimedes.

Oscar Music Productions Ltd., 91 Brick Lane, London, E1 6QN. Tel: 0171 377 6294. Fractal Music for the ST.

Digidesign UK, 3 Alice Court, 116 Putney Bridge Road, London, SW15 2NQ. Tel: 0181 875 9977. Digidesign's own digital audio hardware and software for the PC and Mac.

Digital Music, 27 Leven Close, Chandlers Ford, Hants, SO5 3SH. Tel: 01703 252131. Howling Dog, Dynaware, Musitech. Mainly PC.

EMR, 14 Mount Close, Wickford, Essex, SS11 8HG. Tel: 01702 335747. EMR software for the Acorn Archimedes.

Et Cetera, Et Cetera, Unit 17, Hardman's Business Centre, Rawtenstall, Rossendale, Lancashire, BB4 6HH. Tel: 01706 228039. Blue Ribbon, AL Digital, Turtle Beach, 12 Tone Systems, Musicware, Music Quest.

Fractal Music Ltd., PO Box 1938, Hornsey, London, N8 7DZ.Tel: 0171 272 7482. Fractal Music Composer for the ST.

Gallant, 8 Church Square, Leighton Buzzard, Beds LU7 7AE. Tel: 01525 372621. Goldstar.

Harman International, Unit 2, Boreham Ind Park, Rowley Lane, Borehamwood, Herts., WD6 5PZ. Tel:0181 207 5050. Steinberg.

Intrinsic Technology, 4 Auckland Court, London, SE27 9PE. Tel: 0181 761 0178. Intrinsic's SLAM sample librarian for the ST.

Key Audio Systems Ltd., Unit D, 37 Robjohn's Road, Chelmsford, Essex, CM1 3AG. Tel: 01245 344001. Dr. T.

Klemm Music Technology, PO Box 4 , Arlesy, Beds., SG15 6AA. Tel: 01462 733310. Mark of the Unicorn.

Lowrie Woolf Associates Ltd., Spirella Building, Letchworth, Hertfordshire, SG6 4ET. Tel: 01462 484707. Lowrie Woolf's SeqWin multimedia sequencer for the PC.

MCMXCIX, 9 Hatton Street, London, NW8 8PR. Tel: 0181 963 0663. Opcode, Coda, OSC.

Meridian Software Distribution, East House, East Road Industrial Estate, East Road, London, SW19 1AH. Tel: 0181 543 3500. Blue Ribbon software for the Amiga.

Newtronic, 62b Manor Avenue, London, SE4 1TE. Tel: 0181 691

1087. Geerdes, EMC, Y-Not, DVPI.

PC Services, 78 Beckenham Road, Beckenham, Kent, BR3 4RH. Tel: 0181 658 7251. Sunrise software for the PC.

Roland (UK), Rye Close, Ancells Business Park, Fleet, Hampshire, GU13 8UY. Tel: 01252 816181. Mac and PC hardware and software bundles

Sibelius Software, 75 Burleigh Street, Cambridge, CB1 1DJ. Tel: 01223 302765. Sibelius 6 and 7, professional scorewriting programs for the Acorn Archimedes.

Software Technology Ltd., 40 Princess Street, Manchester, M1 6DE. Tel: 0161 236 2515. Software Technology sequencers and editors for the ST and Amiga.

Sound Technology Plc, 15 Letchworth Point, Letchworth, Herts, SG6 1ND. Tel: 01462 480000. Emagic, Mark of the Unicorn, Goldstar.

Titan Designs, Institute Of Research And Development, University Of Birmingham, Research Park, Vincent Drive, Birmingham, B15 2SQ. Tel: 0121 415 4155. Take Control, Music DTP for the ST.

Yamaha Media Technology, Sherbourne Drive, Tilbrook, Milton Keynes, MK7 8BL. Tel: 01908 366700. Mac and PC hardware and software bundles.

Other useful contacts

Philip Rees, Unit 2 Clarendon Court, Park Street, Charlesbury, Oxford, OX7 3PT. Tel: 01608 811215. Manufacturers of a wide range of excellent MIDI boxes.

Club Cubase, 26 Brunswick Park Gardens, New Southgate, London, N11 1EJ. Tel: 0181 368 2245. THE club for users of Steinberg's seminal program.

20 *Techie stuff*

Decimal to hexadecimal conversion table

Dec	Hex	Dec	Hex	Dec	Hex	Dec	Hex
0	0	32	20	64	40	96	60
1	1	33	21	65	41	97	61
2	2	34	22	66	42	98	62
3	3	35	23	67	43	99	63
4	4	36	24	68	44	100	64
5	5	37	25	69	45	101	65
6	6	38	26	70	46	102	66
7	7	39	27	71	47	103	67
8	8	40	28	72	48	104	68
9	9	41	29	73	49	105	69
10	A	42	2A	74	4A	106	6A
11	B	43	2B	75	4B	107	6B
12	C	44	2C	76	4C	108	6C
13	D	45	2D	77	4D	109	6D
14	E	46	2E	78	4E	110	6E
15	F	47	2F	79	4F	111	6F
16	10	48	30	80	50	112	70
17	11	49	31	81	51	113	71
18	12	50	32	82	52	114	72
19	13	51	33	83	53	115	73
20	14	52	34	84	54	116	74
21	15	53	35	85	55	117	75
22	16	54	36	86	56	118	76
23	17	55	37	87	57	119	77
24	18	56	38	88	58	120	78
25	19	57	39	89	59	121	79
26	1A	58	3A	90	5A	122	7A
27	1B	59	3B	91	5B	123	7B
28	1C	60	3C	92	5C	124	7C
29	1D	61	3D	93	5D	125	7D
30	1E	62	3E	94	5E	126	7E
31	1F	63	3F	95	5F	127	7F

Control change numbers

No	Function	No	Function
0	Bank select	75	Undefined / reverb
1	Modulation wheel	76	Undefined / delay
2	Breath controller	77	Undefined / pitch trans
3	Undefined	78	Undefined / flange or chor
4	Foot controller	79	Undefined / special effects
5	Portamento time	80 -83	General purpose 5-8
6	Data entry	84	Portamento control
7	Main volume	85-90	Undefined
8	Balance	91	Effects depth (effect 1)
9	Undefined	92	Tremolo depth (effect 2)
10	Pan	93	Chorus depth (effect 3)
11	Expression	94	Celeste depth (effect 4)
12	Effect control 1	95	Phaser depth (effect 5)
13	Effect control 2	96	Data increment
14-15	Undefined	97	Data decrement
16-19	General purpose 1-4	98	Non-reg para no LSB
20 -31	Undefined	99	Non-reg para no MSB
32-63	LSB for cont changes 0 – 31	100	Reg para no LSB
64	Damper/ sustain pedal	101	Reg para no MSB
65	Portamento	102-19	Undefined
66	Sostenuto	120	All sound off
67	Soft pedal	121	Reset all controllers
68	Legato footswitch	122	Local control
69	Hold 2	123	All notes off
70	Sound variation / exciter	124	Omni mode off
71	Harmonic content / compr	125	Omni mode on
72	Release time / distortion	126	Mono mode on
73	Attack time / equaliser	127	Poly mode on
74	Brightness /exp or n.gate		

General MIDI drum map

No	Drum sound	No	Drum sound	No	Drum sound
35	Acous bass drum	51	Ride cymbal 1	67	High agogo
36	Bass drum 1	52	Chinese cymbal	68	Low agogo
37	Side stick	53	Ride bell	69	Cabasa
38	Acoustic snare	54	Tambourine	70	Maracas
39	Hand clap	55	Splash cymbal	71	Short whistle
40	Electric snare	56	Cowbell	72	Long whistle
41	Low floor tom	57	Crash cymbal 2	73	Short guiro
42	Closed hi-hat	58	Vibraslap	74	Long guiro
43	High floor tom	59	Ride cymbal 2	75	Claves
44	Pedal hi-hat	60	High bongo	76	High woodblock
45	Low tom	61	Low bongo	77	Low woodblock
46	Open hi-hat	62	Mute hi conga	78	Mute cuica
47	Low mid tom	63	Open hi conga	79	Open cuica
48	High mid tom	64	Low Conga	80	Mute triangle
49	Crash cymbal	65	High timbale	81	Open triangle
50	High tom	66	Low timbale		

General MIDI program change numbers

No	Instrument	No	Instrument
1	Acoustic grand piano	23	Harmonica
2	Bright acoustic piano	24	Tango accordion
3	Electric grand piano	25	Acoustic guitar (nylon)
4	Honky-tonk piano	26	Acoustic guitar (steel)
5	Electric piano 1	27	Electric guitar (jazz)
6	Electric piano 2	28	Electric guitar (clean)
7	Harpsichord	29	Electric guitar (muted)
8	Clavi	30	Overdriven guitar
9	Celesta	31	Distortion guitar
10	Glockenspiel	32	Guitar harmonics
11	Music box	33	Acoustic bass
12	Vibraphone	34	Electric bass (finger)
13	Marimba	35	Electric bass (pick)
14	Xylophone	36	Fretless bass
15	Tubular bells	37	Slap bass 1
16	Dulcimer	38	Slap bass 2
17	Drawbar organ	39	Synth bass 1
18	Percussive organ	40	Synth bass 2
19	Rock organ	41	Violin
20	Church organ	42	Viola
21	Reed organ	43	Cello
22	Accordion	44	Contrabass

No	Instrument	No	Instrument
45	Tremolo strings	87	Lead 7 (fifths)
46	Pizzicato strings	88	Lead 8 (bass + lead)
47	Orchestral harp	89	Pad 1 (new age)
48	Timpani	90	Pad 2 (warm)
49	String ensemble 1	91	Pad 3 (polysynth)
50	String ensemble 2	92	Pad 4 (choir)
51	SynthStrings 1	93	Pad 5 (bowed)
52	SynthStrings 2	94	Pad 6 (metallic)
53	Choir aahs	95	Pad 7 (halo)
54	Voice oohs	96	Pad 8 (sweep)
55	Synth voice	97	FX 1 (rain)
56	Orchestra hit	98	FX 2 (soundtrack)
57	Trumpet	99	FX 3 (crystal)
58	Trombone	100	FX 4 (atmosphere)
59	Tuba	101	FX 5 (brightness)
60	Muted trumpet	102	FX 6 (goblins)
61	French horn	103	FX 7 (echoes)
62	Brass section	104	FX 8 (sci-fi)
63	SynthBrass 1	105	Sitar
64	SynthBrass 2	106	Banjo
65	Soprano sax	107	Shamisen
66	Alto sax	108	Koto
67	Tenor sax	109	Kalimba
68	Baritone sax	110	Bagpipe
69	Oboe	111	Fiddle
70	English horn	112	Shanai
71	Bassoon	113	Tinkle bell
72	Clarinet	114	Agogo
73	Piccolo	115	Steel drums
74	Flute	116	Woodblock
75	Recorder	117	Taiko drum
76	Pan flute	118	Melodic tom
77	Blown bottle	119	Synth drum
78	Shakuhachi	120	Reverse cymbal
79	Whistle	121	Guitar fret noise
80	Ocarina	122	Breath noise
81	Lead 1 (square)	123	Seashore
82	Lead 2 (sawtooth)	124	Bird tweet
83	Lead 3 (calliope)	125	Telephone ring
84	Lead 4 (chiff)	126	Helicopter
85	Lead 5 (charang)	127	Applause
86	Lead 6 (voice)	128	Gunshot

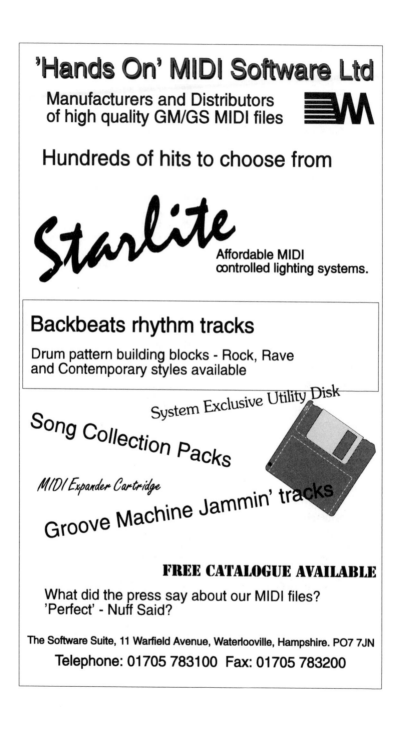

Index

Essential MIDI accessories

You can avoid plugging and unplugging MIDI cables with our switch boxes. The **5S** is a selector with five positions. The **9S** has nine positions and the **2S** has two. The **3B** is a three-into-two changeover unit.

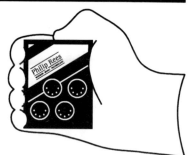

Our **MLD** and bidirectional **MTR** MIDI line driver systems overcome the 15m limit of standard MIDI hardware.

You can't combine MIDI datastreams by joining wires together, so you may need a merge unit - we make the best!

The versatile **TS1** can sync a MIDI sequencer to almost any tape machine.

MDS synchronises your classic drum machines to MIDI clocks. **MCV** lets your MIDI system control your old analogue synths.

Functional simplicity

Some of your MIDI gear may lack Thru sockets. Chains of more than three MIDI devices can suffer from data corruption. You can solve these problems at low cost with popular *Philip Rees'* MIDI thru units.

The **V3** is a battery-powered one-into-three thru box. The **V8**, which has two Ins and eight Outs, needs an external mains adaptor. The **V10** is a mains-powered one-into-ten unit. The mains-powered **W5** dual input thru box has independent source selection for each of its five outputs.

Our products are all made in Britain and express our ideals of reliability and functional simplicity. All our products carry a serious five-year guarantee.

Philip Rees
MODERN MUSIC TECHNOLOGY

Charlbury (01608) 811215
Fax (01608) 811227

Philip Rees, Unit 2, Clarendon Court
Park Street, Charlbury, OXFORD OX7 3PT

twiddly•**b**its

Licks and tricks as MIDI Files

"Their feel has no equal, inspiring to say the least" *Sound on Sound.* Vol 1

"Invaluable. There's currently nothing like it on the market" *Atari ST Review.* Vol 1.

"A brilliant utility" *Keys Germany.* Vol 1.

"Stunning, pushing the fluency of MIDI to a new high" *Future Music.* Vol 3.

"Unbelievably realistic" *The Mix.* Vol 3.

Don't take these reviewer's quotes as gospel. Listen to the demo files and discover yourself the real secret of successful sequencing!

Volume One	General Instruments	£19.95
Volume Two	Gate Effects	£12.95
Volume Three	Electric and Acoustic Guitars	£19.95
Volume Four	Drums and Percussion	£19.95
Twiddly Beats	Volume One Brazilian Rhythms	£19.95
Twiddly Beats	Pre-mapped Brazilian samples available in Roland 750 and Akai Formats	£16.95

KEYFAX SOFTWARE
**PO Box 4408, Henley on Thames, Oxon RG9 1FS
Telephone (01734) 471382**
•

Please add £2.00 for U.K. package and postage.

Other books from PC Publishing

Practical MIDI Handbook 3ed – RA Penfold • 144 pp • ISBN 1 870775 36 8 • £9.95

- Covers General MIDI
- Completely updated
- Covers use of sequencers and computers
- Straightforward non-mathematical introduction to MIDI
- Glossary of MIDI terms

This third edition of our most successful book has been completely revised and updated and now includes a new chapter on General MIDI.

I would certainly recommend the book UKMA MIDI Monitor
Recommended Home & Studio Recording
An informative book Keyboard Player

MIDI Survival Guide – Vic Lennard • 96pp • ISBN 1 870775 28 7 • £7.95

- Over 40 cabling diagrams
- How to budget and buy secondhand
- Using switch, thru and merger boxes
- Transfer songs between different sequencers
- Get the best out of General MIDI
- Understand MIDI implementation charts

Whether you're a beginner or a seasoned pro, the MIDI Survival Guide shows you the way. No maths, no MIDI theory - just practical advice on starting up, setting up and ending up with a working MIDI system.

Fast Guide to Cubase – Simon Millward • 132 pp • ISBN 1870775 49 X • £10.95

- For PC, Atari and Mac
- Get up to speed quickly
- Covers all the essential elements
- Smart move shortcuts
- Save hours of manual searching
- With hands-on projects

Provides an easy way into the essentials of MIDI sequencing using Cubase. The concise text and clear illustrations will save you hours of wading throught the manual and cut down the bewilderment felt by many first time users of the program.

Order form

Please supply

Prac MIDI Handbook _____ copies at £9.95

MIDI Survival Guide _____ copies at £7.95

Fast Guide to Cubase _____ copies at £10.95

I enclose a cheque for £ _____ payable to PC Publishing. Add £2.00 for P&P. (£2.50 overseas)

Or please debit my credit card:

Card no _____

Exp date _____

Signed _____

Name _____

Address _____

_____

_____

_____

_____

Date _____

PC Publishing

Export House, 130 Vale Road, Tonbridge TN9 1SP · Tel 01732 770893 · Fax 01732 770268